How to Remodel
and
Enlarge Your Home

How to Remodel and Enlarge Your Home

By M. E. Daniels

BOBBS-MERRILL

Indianapolis/New York

Designed by Bernard Schleifer
Manufactured in the United States of America

FIRST PRINTING

Library of Congress Cataloging in Publication Data

Daniels, Marie E
  How to remodel and enlarge your home.

  Includes index.
  1. Dwellings—Remodeling. I. Title.
TH4816.D29   643′.7   77-15443
ISBN 0-672-52304-3

CONTENTS

How to Remodel
and
Enlarge Your Home

I

What You Should Know Before You Start

1

MORE HOUSE FOR LESS MONEY

It costs a lot less to build a room than to buy a new house—which accounts for the increasing popularity of add-ons. And examples are plentiful. Of the twenty-six houses along a typical suburban road (where some of the photos in this book were taken) twelve have had rooms added. Eleven have added decks and patios for greater outdoor living space. And nine have lawn storage sheds to eliminate garage and basement clutter. Most of the work was done by the homeowners and their families, in some instances, with professional help.

ADDING WITHOUT ADDING: REMODELING YOUR EXISTING LIVING SPACE

If you plan to join the ranks of the home-expanders, give plenty of thought to determining just how much added living space you really need, and try not to cling to a fixed idea. Decide whether you really need more *room,* or more *rooms*. The difference might amount to a great deal of money. If, for example, you need an extra bedroom, you may be able to get it by dividing a large master bedroom into two rooms by building a partition wall and an extra doorway. You lose a little luxury, but you save a lot of money. When this approach is feasible the job can often be done in a weekend or two for a fraction of the cost of building an addition. As your house remains the same overall size, your heating bill remains virtually the same. And (depending on local regulations) your tax bill may also remain the same.

Other methods include other tricks, too, for gaining a room without actually adding it. An unfinished basement at garage level, for instance, very often becomes a storeroom for everything from bikes and garden tools to power mowers, snow blowers, and leftover lumber and pipe from other projects. The most economical way to free that basement space for conversion to a family room may be simply a matter of buying or building a lawn storage shed. Your house is more livable but no bigger, and in numerous localities your tax is no bigger, if the shed is within a prescribed price limit. These and many other methods of altering typical floor plans to gain a room (even a bathroom) are described and diagrammed in Part II of this book. In chapter 9 you'll find details on buying and building storage sheds.

MAKING THE HOUSE BIGGER WITHOUT ADDING NEW FOUNDATIONS

Often, of course, there just isn't enough living space to divide up for extra rooms. Then the answer lies in adding on. But here too you may be able to save money without compromising on your needs, by using imagination in what you add and where you add it. If, like many of today's homes, yours has a basement garage, you can get a major increase in living space at minimum cost by adding a carport. Then you replace the garage door with a wall, windows that suit your new room and siding to match the house, and convert the garage to living space. But save that overhead door. If you plan for it, you can enclose the carport later (when your budget permits) to make it a full-fledged garage with the same door as the original. What you save by not buying a new door will go a long way toward the price of materials for enclosing the carport or finishing your new living space. The carport requires less material and costs much less to build than a garage or an added room, yet you get your extra room by walling over the original garage doorway. Then, unless the added living space is needed immediately, you can finish it in easy stages for cash and save the cost of interest on a loan, a point to keep in mind for any add-on project where it's possible. Photos and construction drawings later in the book show you just how these garage and carport conversions are made.

MAKING THE HOUSE BIGGER, INCLUDING NEW FOUNDATIONS

Converting a garage to living space, however, is often not the answer. If you want a formal dining room you certainly don't want it in the basement with the kitchen on the floor above. Nor is the basement a frequently chosen location for permanent bedrooms. So in many situations you simply build the room or rooms you want where you want them, from the ground foundation up. If you've never done any major building work, you may find it simpler than you thought it was. If not, you can hire professionals for the job or for the parts of the job you don't want to do yourself. Quite a few homeowner-builders of add-ons have the hard work of foundation building done by professionals and take over the job from there on, as most of us enjoy carpentry. The chapters that follow explain how it's all done. There are simple basic rules for building foundations, floors, walls and roofs. Once you're familiar with these rules you can build to almost any size and shape you like. In a way, it all goes together somewhat like a giant Erector set. But to work with a feeling of confidence, if you haven't had building experience, take the time to read this entire book before you start planning or building.

ADDING PREFABS AND MODULES

One other possibility to look into while you're still in the planning stage is that of the ready-made building that might serve as your addition. Large lumberyards and building suppliers often handle prefabricated garages and other small buildings that, with some preplanning, might be joined to an existing house. There are also prefabricated-home manufacturers (mentioned in later chapters) whose products are often used as add-ons. And finally, there's the professional building mover. He can lift an existing building from its foundation, carry it for miles on a special trailer truck, and set it down on a prepared foundation elsewhere—sometimes as an addition to an existing house. This kind of moving has been done many times, but it calls for careful planning. It can be surprisingly reasonable in price if there are no complications—and the building mover can usually spot these in advance.

There's another type of work the building mover can do that may be extremely important in some small-lot situations where zoning regulations make it impossible to expand a house horizontally in any direction. Here, the building mover can literally "raise the roof" to make it possible to expand the house straight up. Using a high-boom derrick after the topmost wall structure of the house has been cut through, he actually lifts the roof off of the house while pre-readied extension framing is fastened in place to add another story and re-anchor the roof. This, understandably, is a job for professionals, though the homeowner can sometimes cut costs by working with them.

A PREVIEW OF YOUR ENLARGED HOUSE

However you add to your house, you're likely to be concerned with what it will look like after the job is completed. In chapter 10 you'll find a photographic trick that lets you see a picture of the finished addition job even before you start work on it. But try to have someone take a few snapshots of the work as it progresses—and make sure you're in them if you're working on the project. Then, when it's all done, you'll always be able to prove you did it yourself.

2

ABOUT CODES AND TAXES

The first step is to familiarize yourself with the codes that govern what you can do (and how you must do it) and what you cannot do in the locality where you live. Usually there are four codes: zoning, building, electrical and plumbing. They are designed to help you in many and usually all of your projects. They protect you and your neighborhood and can save you money and time. Copies of the codes are usually available free or for a small fee from your building inspector's office. In any event, it is worthwhile to get copies for your own use, as they contain much useful information that can prevent making costly mistakes in your project. If your town or community does not have printed codes, look for them in a nearby town that does, and use those as a guide if you do the work yourself. If you hire a professional to do it for you, he should know the code.

ZONING CODES

These may be very restrictive in some areas, lenient in others. Their overall pur-

pose is to keep the atmosphere and sometimes even the style of a neighborhood safeguarded from unsightly structures or unwise use of property. For example, an addition that suits your needs but comes too close to your neighbor's house for admission of sufficient light and air would be unwise and might be illegal. The same would hold true if your neighbor were to add a room that deprived you of the same advantages. One important type of zoning regulations are those called "setbacks." They specify exactly how far your house must be from side, front and rear boundaries of your property. When extending your home at ground level seems the only solution you can live with, and your planned addition would go over the bounds set by your local zoning code, you may apply for a "variance." Usually, in this case, the zoning commission will hold a hearing so that you may state your case, and your neighbors may express their feelings in the matter. Usually a compromise can be reached, and often there are no objections at all. This is especially true if your addition will add to the appearance of your home and to the street where you live.

BUILDING CODES

These specify structural requirements, such as the sizes of rafters, joists, headers and lintels over windows and doors, for specific spans. This type of information is usually in the form of charts which make everything clear and simple. As they have been worked out with safety and sound, durable construction in mind, they are very helpful all the way through your project. Also, when you know the sizes and types of construction materials you will be required to use, you have a sound basis for figuring your costs if you do the work yourself, and you will have working knowledge of the situation if you hire a professional for some or all of the work. Although codes vary from one area to another, often from one town to the next one, you'll have to follow the one that applies to your particular community.

Building codes also have specifics about foundations, how thick the masonry must be, whether pier foundations are permitted, footing sizes required and other details. The code will also tell you how deep you have to go for your footings to avoid frost heave or undue settling.

PLUMBING CODES

These govern any piping that carries water into a house and the waste pipes that carry it out to sewer or septic system. The kinds of pipe permitted are also specified (copper, plastic, iron, etc.). This varies widely from one locality to another. Often, specific types are allowed for certain purposes but not for others. Some codes require that all the waste material from the plumbing system be discharged into the

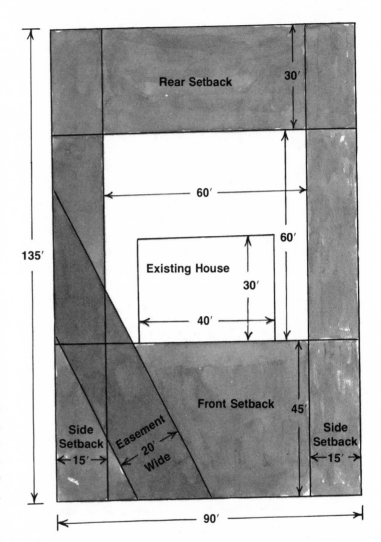

Fig. 1. How setbacks and easements can affect your add-on plans. Here, a 90' x 135' building lot provides a permissible building area of 60' x 60', with one corner cut off by an easement. The shaded portions are non-building areas, the white portions are permissible building areas. There's ample area to the rear of the house in this example. Check all regulations pertaining to your property before you make your add-on plans.

septic system, if you have one, rather than a public sewer. Other codes require that the waste from such fixtures as showers, tubs, sinks, etc., be discharged into a separate "dry well," to avoid overloading the septic system. (A dry well is an excavation filled with crushed stone or small rocks that dissipates waste water or effluent into the soil.) Regulations in some areas require that all plumbing be done by a licensed plumber; others allow the homeowner to install the water supply system. If you are permitted to do the work yourself, an inspection is often required. *Don't cover the plumbing system with your interior wall until the inspection has been made.*

ELECTRICAL CODES

These tell you what you can and cannot do in the wiring of your home, with the safety of the building and its occupants in mind. The National Electrical Code is available from electrical suppliers and the National Fire Protection Association, 60 Battery March St., Boston, Mass. 02110. Check on the price before you order it by mail. This is the basis for many local codes, though they may differ from it in numerous ways. However, if there is a *local* code where you live, it takes precedence over the National Code. In some areas only a licensed electrician is allowed to do any of the wiring. In others, the homeowner may do it, providing he follows the code and his work passes the inspection. As with

plumbing, *the electrical work must be left exposed for inspection before the interior wall is put up.*

TAXES

Taxes on your addition can often be estimated in advance. In some instances, you can find out by calling the tax assessor's office, stating the expected cost of the job. In some areas, certain items, like a fireplace, add a fixed amount to your overall assessment. Many towns place a higher assessment on tiled baths than on those where a waterproof panel board is used. It pays to find out as much as you can before you finish your plans, so you won't be shocked by your next tax bill. Of course, these considerations can be outweighed by the degree of luxury you have set your heart on, and there may not be too much difference anyway.

EASEMENTS

Check your property deed to make sure there is no easement that would prohibit you from placing your addition just where you would like it. An easement gives another party the right to use part of your property. This might be a right-of-way for a utility company to lay cables or water mains across some part of your property, with the right to come on that part of the property for repair and maintenance work.

II

Remodeling Your Existing Living Space

3

HOW TO PLAN ON PAPER

As mentioned in chapter 1, the problem of inadequate living space can sometimes be solved by methods that cost less than actually enlarging the house. So it pays to check into these possibilities carefully as a first step. In the following six chapters, the essentials of these methods are given one by one. You are the analyst on the job and the decision maker. When you can estimate the cost and working time likely to be involved in each method, you can decide whether to remodel your existing living space or add to it. Whichever you do, you're likely to spend far less than you would if you moved to a new and larger house. And you avoid the costs and headaches of moving.

If there's a chance of adding rooms to your house simply by dividing large rooms into smaller ones by means of partition walls, your imagination is the first tool to use. And don't limit it unnecessarily. Think not only in terms of room sizes but also of furniture types and sizes that make smaller rooms practical. When the added rooms are for children, as is very often the case, the reduced size presents less of a problem. Bunk beds, for example, are well liked by children and provide sleeping space for two in about half the floor area required by twin beds. And the cost of a partition wall plus the bunk beds is far less than that of an addition to a house, built from the ground up. In the material that follows, you'll find both specific and general guidelines to make your planning easier and help you avoid the common pitfalls.

There are several simple ways to make penciled scale diagrams of your rooms, pieces of furniture or the floor plan of your entire house. (Do all this well in advance of the actual building job.) The term "scale" simply means that the dimensions are *proportionally* reduced or "scaled down" in the diagrams. Typically, a half inch in the drawing might equal a foot in the actual room dimensions. Thus, a 12′-wide room would be 6″ wide on your penciled diagram. The scale you use depends on the overall size of whatever you are diagraming and the size of the paper you are using. If you're diagraming an entire house that's 24′ wide and 40′ long, you might use a scale of $1/4″$ to the foot. Your diagram would then be 6″ wide and 10″ long—small enough to draw on standard typewriter paper. And you can make the job especially easy by using graph paper, which is usually available from stationery stores with a gridwork of ¼″ squares printed on it. You can also use an architect's scale rule, sometimes called a mechanical engineer's scale rule or just plain scale rule. These rules (triangular in cross section) are also available from stationery stores. They are marked in inches along one edge and in various scales, such as ³/₃₂″ to the foot, ³/₁₆″, and up to as much as 3″ to the foot on other edges. Typically, each scale also has one full unit divided into twelfths so you can scale your drawing (where necessary) in "miniature" inches. This scale rule plus a plastic mechanical drawing triangle lets you use plain paper for your scale diagrams. The triangle has a square corner for squaring the corners of your diagrams.

ABOUT THE DOORWAYS IN YOUR DIAGRAMS

When a single room is divided into two, an extra doorway may or may not be required. If you are simply partitioning off an "eat-in" kitchen to make the dining area into a formal dining room, an open archway through the partition is often all that's required. If you are dividing a master bedroom into two small bedrooms, however, you need an extra door and doorway. And the new door should provide entry from a hallway or from some room other than a bedroom. *Do not* plan a bedroom door that requires passing through one bedroom to reach another. This destroys the privacy of both rooms. In most cases, private entry can be arranged fairly easily, often by modifying a closet, as shown in the before-and-after floor plans.

ABOUT PARTITION WALL CONSTRUCTION

A partition wall is built like any other wall in the house, though there can be some difference in framework lumber size. The usual inside partition walls of a house are built with a framework of 2 x 4 lumber. When this is covered on both sides with typical gypsum wallboard, the overall thickness is around 4½″. Where space is tight in later room divisions, however, the partition wall framing may be of 2 x 3 lumber, reducing the wall thickness by an inch, which sometimes is important. Applying paneling directly to the framing without wallboard reduces the wall thickness still further, typically by about an additional ½″. Framing along the wall and around doorways is as shown in chapter 6.

A Problem to Avoid

If you build your partition wall framework on the floor of the room, *do not* make it the full height from floor to ceiling. If you do, you'll find it difficult if not impossible to erect. The explanation lies in the fact that the diagonal dimension of the wall frame, as at the ends, is greater than the height of the wall. So, as you try to erect it, one corner of the base of the wall jams against the floor while the diagonally opposite corner of the top member (plate) of the wall jams against the ceiling. The answer, however, is simple. Build the partition wall framing 1½″ short of full height from floor to ceiling. It can then be erected without jamming, and the 1½″ space filled with an additional 2 x 4 or 2 x 3. The extra piece may be slipped in place either above or below the framework. Usually it's easier to fasten it in place below it. Often it's

Fig. 2. Floor plan of a popular 3-bedroom split-level house design.

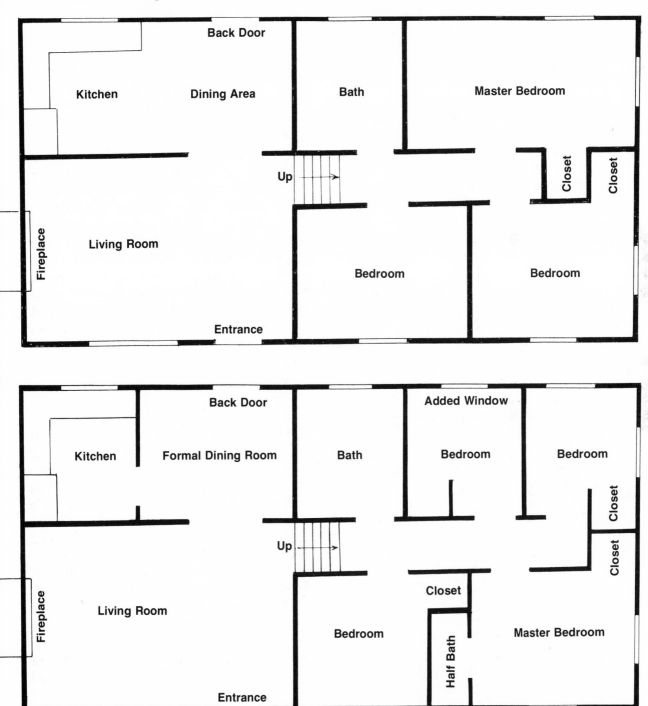

Fig. 3. How the floor plan in the previous diagram can be modified to add a fourth bedroom plus a half bath. A partition wall converts the original master bedroom into two smaller ones. A window is added to ventilate one of them. A closet is shifted to provide an entry way to the other. A second partition wall steals a little space from another bedroom to accommodate the half bath. A partition wall also separates the kitchen from the dining area to create a formal dining room.

nailed down in advance, after which the wall frame is erected and lifted (and nailed) atop the base member. This method enables you to slide the partition framing horizontally into position on the sole that has been nailed to the floor. As the partition framing need not be tilted, it won't jam against the member already nailed to the floor.

When a new partition wall runs parallel to joists, place it so the plate can be nailed along a joist. If the partition runs across the joists, nail it in place to each joist. After locating one of the joists and determining their spacing, this is not difficult.

ABOUT WINDOWS

Room dividing by partition wall sometimes leaves one of the newly created

rooms with all the original windows and the other one with none. This is a relatively minor problem, as an extra window or two can be installed in an outside wall of the windowless room. Check with your lumberyard or building supplier in advance on window sizes. If you select a window width that requires the cutting of only one stud you can do the job without too much work. The procedure begins with cutting an opening in the interior wallboard slightly greater in height than the window size and wide enough to reach to the two outer studs, leaving one stud in the middle. This enables you to cut away a section of the center stud and install a header at the top of the opening, and a sill at the bottom, as shown in chapter 15, for old-type framing. After that the sheathing and siding can be cut out around the perimeter of the opening. The window can then be installed. The opening, of course, should be made to match the window. When you buy your window, examine it, and if you have any questions about installing it, ask for information where you buy it. You want to know in advance what the window opening size should be for an accurate fit.

If you'd prefer to have the window installed by a professional, get a written estimate on the job from several sources, including the price of the window or windows. If you hire someone to do the job, be sure he carries insurance that covers him while working on your house. Your own insurance may not cover people hired to do this type of work. In case of accident (not likely, but possible, especially in work on the second story), you don't want to be the one footing the bill.

Fig. 4. If your remodeling requires added windows, look at them in advance at your lumberyard or building supplier's. You'll find a wide variety of types and sizes including casement and double-hung forms as well as bays and bows. These are Andersen windows. You can usually match your present windows if the house is fairly modern. Get specifications for the exact wall opening size required.

4

ADDING A HALF BATH

When an extra bathroom has a high priority on your list of additions, and you still cannot *expand* your home, consider a half bath. This has a washbasin and a toilet, and takes very little space if all components are measured and custom fitted to the space you have available. The half bath can be the answer to the early morning rush hour when children are off to school and working members of the family have to meet a commuting schedule. Keep in mind that actual baths and showers can be scheduled to meet the needs of family members when there is more leisure time.

Fitting a half bath into an existing house may seem a bit difficult, but it is not if you carefully measure the space you have at your disposal. One simple solution can be a closet. At first you may think this is not feasible or even possible. But measure your closet. If it is two feet deep and five feet long, it can adequately contain both a toilet and basin of one of the standard sizes. Instead of the standard basin, in very cramped space, you can substitute a shiny stainless steel bar sink. This unit is typically only fifteen inches square, with a mixing faucet and basket-type strainer-

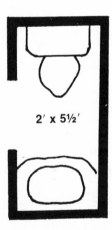

Fig. 5. Half bath can be built in a closet as small as 2' x 5½' inside.

2' x 5½'

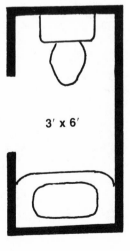

Fig. 6. In 3' x 6' closet, half bath is less cramped.

3' x 6'

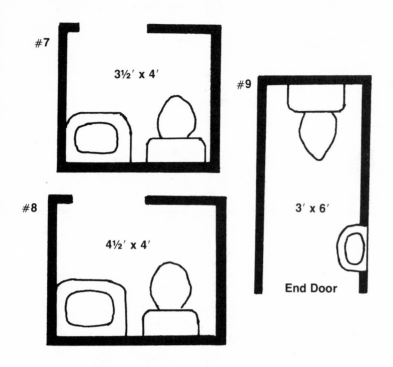

#7

3½' x 4'

#8

4½' x 4'

#9

3' x 6'

End Door

Fig. 7. In 3½' x 4' closet, basin and toilet may be placed side by side.

Fig. 8. Same arrangement as in previous plan is used in this 4' x 4½' closet that allows a little more elbow room.

Fig. 9. When entrance to narrow closet must be through one of the short walls, a bar sink or marine-type sink may be necessary instead of standard lavatory, to allow walk-in clearance.

stopper, and is easily mounted in a shallow counter. Like a standard washbasin, the bar sink is available from plumbing suppliers.

In some cases, you can tie your half bath into your existing soil stack. Sometimes you have to install an additional stack (see chapter 18). These considerations depend on the individual situation and your local code. So when you apply for a building permit for your alteration, discuss these details with the building inspector.

If a half bath tucked into a closet is on an inside wall, as a hallway, and has no

possibility of having a window, a bathroom ventilator, with a light, may be installed in the ceiling and ducted to the outside wall. Some models include an electric heater. Proper switching can give you options for using the appliance in several variations such as light and blower separately, heater and light, or all three, depending on your needs. The ventilator with light is desirable in any case and in some areas may be required by the code when there can be no window.

Important Points About Doors to Half Baths

The direction a door swings to open can be extremely important in close quarters, so plan it in advance. This is especially important where a half bath is built into closet space. As the diagrams show, the best location for the door is in one of the longer walls, between toilet and washbasin. If the door must be located at one end of the closet, you may have to use a marine-type basin designed for the limited space available in smaller cabin boats. You can buy this type from marine suppliers like Defender Industries, Inc., P.O. Box 697, 255 Main Street, New Rochelle, N.Y. 10801. In the smallest common sizes, the marine unit may be as little as 11″ x 13″. This is compact enough to recess into the wall framing between studs to allow extra space to walk past it.

If the closet in which you install your half bath happens to have sliding doors, leave them in place if spacing is suitable. They can serve just as well as hinged doors for your half bath, and they eliminate possible problems, as when a hinged door swings in or out in such a way as to block passage or bump furniture or fixtures.

5

A FORMAL DINING ROOM
FROM AN EAT-IN KITCHEN

While still working in the original living area of your home, give some thought to your living-dining-kitchen area. In many homes, the kitchen is quite large, to accommodate an eating area. When children are grown, however, and a formal dining room is more suitable for your life style, shrink the kitchen so that its eating area contributes space to create a formal dining room. A strategically placed partition may be all that is needed to achieve this, and there are many materials, easy to use for the home handyman (or professional if you decide to use one) with a minimum of time and labor. Translucent panels allow light to filter through from one room to the next, while concealing kitchen clutter from guests in the dining room. Panels of hardboard in open filigree patterns, which come in a wide variety of styles, can be purchased and painted to blend with your room colors. These panels allow light and air to flow through the rooms. Choose one to take care of the situation where air as well as light is desirable. Some patterns are great for concealment, and careful use of lighting and color can make a very effective screen. A light color on the dining room side of the panels tends to reduce visibility through them into the kitchen.

When there is plenty of light and air in the dining room, your options are wide open, depending on your budget. Paneling makes an elegant background in any room, and, since it is pre-finished, there is little to do as far as maintenance is concerned. Paneling has the advantage that pictures and mirrors can be mounted on it with ease. If you want a paneled partition, use simple 2 x 2 framing, as in chapter 3. Use an extra stud (post) if necessary at the point on the wall where you intend to hang a heavy mirror, unless you install a ceiling molding for the purpose. When the wall is to be painted a solid color, gypsum wallboard is cheap and takes an excellent finish. Check with your paint supplier as to whether a wallboard primer is necessary for use with the paint you plan to use. In any of these partition walls, if space is at a premium, the framing may be simply 2 x 3's or 2 x 2's, thus saving both space and money. (Use 2 x 2's for filigree and other light materials.) Always check your code.

Sometimes a new arrangement of cabinets and counters in the kitchen will do more than make this type of remodeling feasible: you may wind up with the bonus of a more workable kitchen. And remember that a "work kitchen" is easier to care for than the large eat-in type. As appliances are closer together, you save steps in the preparation of meals, and will find dining more relaxing for the entire family.

Fig. 10. Here, kitchen has been separated from dining area with partition wall and twin doors to create formal dining room. Franklin stove, though usable, has been painted white as decor feature. Floor covering makes cleaning easy and quick. ARMSTRONG CORK CO.

6

BASEMENT CONVERSIONS

Most basements contain as much square footage of living space as the first floor of the house. Usually part of it is devoted to heating and laundry equipment and, of course, the stairway. But as heat and water are at hand, with a little ingenuity you can transform this area into living space with the added convenience of a bar sink. Furnace and laundry are simply partitioned off. The normal basement clutter of bicycles, unused furniture and similar items can be removed to the partitioned area or to a storage shed. In many areas these sheds, depending on their cost, are not even placed on property tax rolls— check with your assessor before you plan on this. Various types of sheds you can buy or build are shown in the photos in chapter 9.

Basement Ceilings

A tiled ceiling is the easiest and cheapest to install for the do-it-yourselfer. The light-weight tiles are stapled to 1 x 4 strips run at right angles to the joists, nailed to them, and spaced to match the tile size. "Dropped ceiling" systems are suspended a short distance below the ceiling joists and have their own supporting grids, which are attached to the joists. Most are light weight, thus easy to install. The ceiling panels, which come in a variety of textures and tones that require no painting, are also light weight and easy to handle—a prime consideration when you are working over your head. The panels drop neatly into the gridwork. The ceiling, when completed, will conceal the usual plumbing and wiring essentials that are often suspended below the joists. If repairs or additions to the wiring or plumbing are required at a later date, the panels simply lift out for access to these utilities. Inquire at your lumberyard about the types of tiles and grid-and-panel systems for your purpose.

Basement Walls

These may be insulated or not, depending on your climate. Foam insulation can be used against masonry walls. This material comes in panels sized to fit between furring strips attached to the walls. The

Fig. 11. *Typical unfinished basement, used for storage, can become attractive living space.* ARMSTRONG CORK CO.

Fig. 12. *First step in this basement finishing job is at ceiling level. Mounting strips of 1 x 4 are first nailed across ceiling at right angles to joists and spaced to match ceiling tile size. Then ceiling tiles are stapled to strips, as shown. These tiles by Armstrong Cork Co. are sound absorbent acousti-*

cal type. Job goes faster on Mr. and Mrs. basis, as helpers can hand tiles up to whoever works on ladder. ARMSTRONG CORK CO.

Fig. 13. *If floor tiles are laid after ceiling is completed, you avoid chance of marring floor with ladder legs. Tiles being laid are vinyl asbestos. Adhesive used with the tiles can be applied with ordinary paint brush. Using two tile colors, many patterns are possible.* ARMSTRONG CORK CO.

Fig. 14. Result of ceiling and floor tile installation is attractive family room instead of drab basement. Cement paint was used to dress up walls. Note use of drapes below high cellar windows to create effect of larger windows. Methods shown add living area with very little work and expense. ARMSTRONG CORK CO.

foam panels are fastened to the walls with mastic made for the purpose. (Be sure the mastic is matched to the foam you use— the wrong one can destroy the foam.) Paneling, available in many kinds of wood and plastic finishes, nailed to the strips so the joints meet snugly on the strips, makes an attractive, durable, pre-finished wall. Moldings at floor and ceiling make a neat, professional-looking installation. Some of the newer foam-paneling systems can be installed with mastic alone, eliminating the furring strips. Check on their availability at your supplier.

Dressing Up the Basement Stairway

The storage space under the stairs should not be ignored, but the stairway itself will need some dressing up, since it will be part of your living area. Most basement stairs have no risers to close the spaces between the steps. This is a simple carpentry job that should be done where the storage space under the stairs is to be used. It also permits carpeting if that suits your decor.

Various types of wood or metal railings that blend with most decorative themes

Fig. 15. Another unfinished basement and another finishing method. As furnace and oil storage tank are at one end of basement, they must be partitioned off from living space to come. Note girder under joists and overhead pipes. MASONITE CORP.

Fig. 16. Masonite simulated wood paneling is used on basement walls and on framed partitioned wall separating living area from furnace room. It's also used on sides of basement stairway. Louvered door at foot of stairs leads to furnace room, also provides air circulation. Resilient floor covering is used over concrete floor. Dropped ceiling at level of bottom of girder is made up of standard dropped-ceiling panels and ready-made supporting grid-work, both available from lumberyards and building suppliers. Both girder and pipes are concealed by dropped ceiling. MASONITE CORP.

Fig. 17. Furniture can usually remain in the room while partition walls are built. Here, laundry area is being partitioned off from basement family room. Partition wall at right has plate nailed to underside of girder. Wall at left, at right angle to girder, has 4 x 4 plate for rigidity, as top of wall must be located between joists. Job, planned as Christmas present, was started two weekends before holiday.

Fig. 18. Work was completed before holiday in time for Christmas cards to be hung from girder. Walls are covered with paneling to match existing ones.

are available from your local lumberyard. They range from simple balusters supporting wooden railings to slender closet poles that reach from each step to the ceiling. The latter makes an attractive pattern in a modern mood. Metal railings of iron or aluminum in ornate designs create still another atmosphere. Some types can be had by mail order from outlets like Sears.

If you enclose your stairs in solid walls (paneling to match the basement walls), they can be handrail height, ending with a molding to cap the paneling edges, or they can extend to the ceiling. In this case, a simple railing, mounted on brackets made to fit the railing, fills the bill. In any event, railings are a safety factor. Railing brackets are available from hardware stores and building suppliers.

Basement Floors

There are several ways to make the floor of your transformed basement attractive and at the same time give it a durable finish. One of the quickest solutions is to use a paint made for the purpose. These paints come in a variety of colors, not all of them very beautiful, as they were originally developed for strictly utilitarian purposes of making the floor durable, easy to clean and unlikely to smudge. However, if you use two or more colors *of the same brand* so that they are compatible, it is possible to come up with an original blended color of your own that does the

trick for your particular room. Another scheme is to apply a base color, and do a spatter-dash job with another good contrasting color after the base coat is dry. In this method, the "spatter" color is applied by dipping a small, stiff brush (often a toothbrush) into the spatter color. Then the brush is smartly tapped against a rod or board so that the top color is spattered over the base color, leaving a confetti-like pattern. Try this on a scrap panel of leftover material or in an under-stair storage area first. Also, using masking tape to define the areas, you can have stripes, squares, even a shuffleboard or other game layout painted on the old concrete floor.

Synthetic floor coverings, made for use below grade (ground level), can be used directly over a dry concrete floor. (Specify tiles for use on concrete when you buy.) The range of patterns is so wide that there is sure to be one to suit your decor. Just be certain that when you purchase, you get at the same time the proper adhesive (if adhesive is required for your installation) and the proper solvent for clean-up. The tools needed are not expensive and can be used over the years for many other jobs.

Depending on the use of your basement rooms, you may or may not want the luxury of carpeting. Some of the indoor-outdoor types can be used directly on the concrete if your basement is a dry one, but check with your dealer before you purchase or lay it. Carpet can also be used over a vinyl-covered concrete floor, as can throw rugs.

7

THE ATTIC

An unfinished attic is a ready-made extra room. Insulation and finishing to suit your needs are all that is required to transform this family catch-all into attractive living space. You are in luck if the attic is floored over, but if it is not, plywood will make a sturdy floor. The thickness of the plywood you use will depend on your local code requirements and whether you intend to put a finished floor over the plywood or to simply use carpeting.

If an unfinished attic has insulation between the ceiling joists of the room below, it is best to leave it there as a sound barrier and to install new insulation between the roof rafters before installing the ceiling, as described later.

When an attic has small, inadequate windows, there are ways to correct the situation. Dormers are one. This entails some new framing and a portion of new roof, but the dormer can transform a small ill-ventilated room to an airy one and is often worth the effort. Details for framing a dormer are illustrated in chapter 16. Sometimes all that's necessary is larger windows in the gable end walls of the attic. This is much easier and more economical

Fig. 19. Spiral stairs like this are available in kit form for homeowner assembly. This is large version. Smaller models can be used to reach newly finished attic from hallway as narrow as 4'. MYLEN SPIRAL STAIR

than building a dormer. For attic storage, build vertical "knee walls" at the low sides of your rooms, leaving the central portion, where there's full headroom, open for furnishings. In any event, be sure that the entire roof area is *fully* insulated.

The use you intend to make of your attic rooms will, of course, determine the type of wall and ceiling material you will use. Wood paneling and hardboard paneling both come in a variety of wood finishes and more sophisticated forms, and are easy to put up. As they are prefinished, once they are up that is the end of the job. However, if you have a more custom look in mind, use insulating wallboard (to add to your insulation) and wallpaper or paint, or a combination of the two.

Reaching the attic may be an awkward situation when you want to use it for living area. Folding stairs that must be raised into the attic floor from a lower hallway can be an inconvenience, and children can't reach them for pull-down. In any case, they are more utilitarian than decorative. Also, when you have folding stairs, chances are there is not a long enough run of wall to allow the building of a regular stairway. A charming and surprisingly inexpensive solution to this problem is the spiral stair. Available in kit form for the do-it-yourselfer from manufacturers like Mylen Industries Spiral Stair Division, it comes with complete instruction sheets that make the job quick and easy. An entire installation can be ready to use in as little as two hours. A questionnaire from the company shows you how to measure for an exact fit in the space you have. One can be fitted into a hallway not only as a space saver but also for its decorative effect. The address for Mylen Industries is 650 D Washington St., Peekskill, N.Y. 10566.

8

ENCLOSING A PORCH
OR OPEN BREEZEWAY

ENCLOSING A PORCH

Enclosing an existing porch is another way to add to your living space. Properly insulated, and with a small addition to your heating such as an extra radiator or heating duct from your present system, the porch becomes a living area room with a minimum of effort and expense. Depending on its location, the enclosed porch can be adapted to a variety of uses—dining room, guest room, family or TV room. Lawn and garden space can take the place of the porch for outdoor relaxing. The area under the porch, if it's high enough, is ideal, as it's sheltered by the porch. (See Fig. 194.)

ENCLOSING AN OPEN BREEZEWAY

An open breezeway can be converted to almost any type of room you want. If you cherish the open look and the view of lawn and garden from your breezeway, you do not have to sacrifice this effect when enclosing it. Large windows of insulating double glass retain the open feeling. When screened for opening in the warm months, they allow free passage of the breezes you enjoyed when the area was wide open. Allow for enough solid wall space to permit a convenient arrangement for the furniture you want in the room. Many breezeways are located between the garage and the kitchen. This proximity to your water system makes the addition of a bar sink an easy job, if you plan it so that water and waste pipes can be hooked into the existing plumbing. Wiring is, of course, available no matter what room the breezeway adjoins. This is also true of heating. An added radiator or duct, depending on the type of heating system you have, usually would not put a strain on the central heating plant if you insulate the room adequately. If your heating system is a borderline case, a wood stove may be the answer for very cold weather. Combined with a factory-made chimney such as Metlvent, the installation is quick and easy. Also, a wood stove that has a cook-top can save the day when your area suffers a power outage. You can keep warm and cook with the same energy source.

9

HOW TO REGAIN STORAGE SPACE LOST IN REMODELING

STORAGE AND DECOR TIPS

When a half bath is built into a closet, one of the problems you face is finding storage space to replace that of the lost closet. One partial answer is under-bed storage, which may be under a regular bed or bunk beds. Plastic boxes with tight-fitting lids to keep out dust are available in a variety of sizes. Large department stores often stock them. Ask first for a list of sizes and prices, then buy the type that suits your needs best. Also think about storage furniture. A wardrobe that can be placed in a room corner can often replace much of the lost storage space. If you want a full-fledged built-in closet, remember that part of it can be recessed into an existing inside wall. (Outside walls are usually packed with insulation.) Recessing adds about 4″ to the depth of the closet, reducing the distance the closet must extend into the room. If you run your closet pole parallel to the wall, you can plan on a 24″ depth back-to-front, with only 20″ of it actually extending into the room. Thin doors made of ½″ plywood or comparable particle board (from the lumberyard) help minimize the floor space required for the closet. In general, you can figure the outside shoulder-to-shoulder width of clothes on a coat hanger as about 24″. So you can't fit hangers crosswise between studs only 16″ apart in a wall recess. That's why the closet pole should run parallel to the wall. Then with the hanger ends projecting into the spaces between studs, you can hang a dozen or more articles of clothing, including overcoats, in each 16″ space.

If your room division or closet–half-bath job results in a squeezed-in effect in a bedroom, remember that a light wall color tends to make a room look bigger. Also try large mirrors on opposite walls. A door mirror on the outside of the half-bath door can contribute to the effect. In a room occupied by young children, where mirror breakage is a possibility, you can use mirrored Mylar® plastic. For your nearest source of this mirrored sheet material look in the Yellow Pages of your local phone book under "Plastics."

BUY OR BUILD A SHED

If finishing your basement, attic or garage has left you without a place to store bicycles, unused furniture or other normal household clutter, a shed may be the answer.

Fig. 20. You can buy a metal shed similar to this one from mail order houses like Sears and Montgomery Ward, and many lumberyards and building suppliers. They're usually sold "knocked down" for assembly by the buyer, according to instructions included. Typical sizes range from 5' x 6' to 9' x 10' and larger, including some as large as 14' x 19'.

Fig. 21. Wooden types like this can be bought ready to assemble at many lumberyards, or they can be built from scratch if you're experienced at plain everyday carpentry. This one is owner-built. Framing is generally similar to that shown in chapter 6, but stud spacing is often 24" on centers.

Fig. 22. If your home is an old traditional one you can build a storage shed to match it, like this. Favor a rambling design common in very old out-buildings. Follow framing methods in chapters 14–16. To simplify the job you can use panel-type board-and-batten-style siding. One form is grooved plywood. Other board-and-batten panels are made in hardboard. You can also use rough sawn boards (available at many lumberyards), like these. Horizontal sections of 2 x 4 should then be nailed between studs near their midpoint to serve as nailing strips for board midpoints. Battens of 1 x 2 are nailed on after boards are up. If shed is to be heated (as for a workshop) use plywood sheathing with siding over it (see chapter 15) and insulate.

Fig. 23. If your house is genuine early American and has a barn or other outbuilding on the property, it may be possible to make more complete use of it. This outbuilding, more than 180 years old, serves as a 2-car garage. Inside stairway to loft (now used for storage) was removed to provide car space. New stairway built on outside leads to loft door, also serves to display potted plants in summer. Same outside stair system can be used in new construction to provide maximum usable interior space at ground level plus easy access to upper-level storage area.

Fig. 24. Lawn building at pond's edge has enclosed lockable 10' x 12' storage section at left, open-sided roofed cookout dining area on right. Attractive, economical and relatively easy to build by methods shown starting in chapter 11. Plan size according to your needs.

Fig. 25. Adding a shed to a shed. Refuse cans kept in original plywood shed made it necessary to store bikes and larger garden tools in already cramped garage. Low shed attached to original one solves the problem. It's framed with 2 x 4 lumber with studs spaced for plywood doors wide enough for refuse cans. Here, at start of job, can is used as size guide. Horizontal front plate is nailed to top of studs, short plate runs back to studs nailed to shed wall.

Fig. 26. Horizontal 2 x 4 header is nailed to side of shed with upper edge high enough to provide outward and downward roof slope of 1" per foot.

Fig. 27. Rafters of 2 x 4 lumber, mounted with wide faces up, are nailed from header to plate on 16" centers.

Fig. 28. After rafters are decked with $1/2$" plywood, roof is covered with roll roofing. Roofing strips are laid from lower edge of roof upward, with upper strip overlapping edge of lower strip by 2". Roofing nails are used about 3" apart along edges of roofing and at seam. Seam and all nail heads are covered with troweling-consistency asphalt roofing cement, applied with putty knife.

Fig. 29. Completed add-on shed has barn-style diagonals on doors. Battens on wall of original shed complete the effect.

III

How to Make Your House Bigger

10

PLANNING YOUR ADDITION

If you have a surveyor's map of your property, make a tracing of it (on tracing paper from an art supply store) and draw an outline of your house on it (see Fig. 1, p. 15). You can get the position of the house by measuring from it to the property boundaries. If your property corners aren't marked by iron pipes (driven by the surveyor) or other markers, such as stone marker posts, try to locate the surveyor who did the original job. Ask him what he'd charge to provide you with such markers. Sometimes, too, your next door neighbor on one side or the other will know where the markers are—they're often in place but not too easy to find. If you have no map of your property, you can usually get a copy from the town or city offices. Start with the tax assessor's office. It may take a few calls, but you'll finally be referred to the right department. This routine varies with the locality, but a few local phone calls usually do the trick. The procedure may seem like a lot of fuss, but it's important, because it's necessary to keep within the setbacks. If you go beyond the allowed limits, you can end up with serious problems. At this stage, it's a good idea to ask your friendliest neighbors what they know about the general procedure—especially neighbors who have added to their homes.

THE FIRST STEP

Once you have your map with your house outlined on it (the map you get from the town may not show the house), you're ready to begin. You can use taut string between the corner markers to get your property outline and measure inward to the house to get its outline. Then you can draw it on your map. But do it carefully.

YOUR PRESENT HOUSE

Begin by measuring the floor plan of your present house, room by room. You can do this on graph paper, letting the squares indicate inches or feet, depending on their size. The graph paper also keeps your floor plan squared. Then use the same graph paper to outline the floor plan of your addition, and add about a foot at the setback end of the outline to allow leeway for the outside wall thickness. If you find your planned addition comes too close to the boundary line, try reshaping it. Often you can shift the dimensions of a room so that the narrow measurement runs parallel to the boundary line to keep your plan within the setback. Or you can revise the dimensions of the entire addition. Use your imagination. In most cases, there's no real problem.

ROOM SHIFTING

Where there is a problem, you can sometimes overcome it by room shifting. If you plan to add a bedroom on the bedroom wing of your house (many houses have all bedrooms on one side) and you find that the extra room will bring you too close to the boundary, think about rearranging things. Maybe you can add a new dining room on the other side (assuming there's more property room there) and use the old dining room as a bedroom—with some modifications, maybe a partition. Possibilities like this aren't always apparent at first glance, but they show up when you give them some thought. Often, too, there's more room at the back of the property than at the sides. Some room shifting may make an addition at the back feasible. All this, of course, is necessary only in tight situations. You may have ample room for your addition on all sides.

Another possibility to consider is that of shifting rooms that you have always considered as "locked in." The kitchen is often thought of this way. As its plumbing is relatively simple, however, it can often

be moved without prohibitive expense. If there's no other answer, however, give it some thought. If you don't think you'd like to do the plumbing alterations yourself, have a professional plumber look it over and give you an estimate on what you have in mind. Generally speaking, it's wise to skip the idea of moving a bathroom because of the larger drainage system involved.

REMEMBER STANDARD BUILDING MATERIAL SIZES

Once you've determined the location and size of your addition, think about its construction in terms of material modules. You'll save money. For example, you'll undoubtedly be using plywood sheathing on the outside of your addition. So plan the addition's outside dimensions to use standard 4' x 8' plywood panels. For example, if you make a wall 24' long, you can use six 4'-wide panels to cover it with sheathing. If you want the room a little bigger, make it either 28' (which calls for one more panel) or 26' (which calls for half a panel). Remember that when you use half a panel on the front wall, you can use the other half on the back wall, so there's no waste. The object is to think in modular terms for the sake of economy. You can't eliminate waste altogether, but you can hold it down. Naturally, the inside of your addition has to be smaller than the outside, and the inside wallboard have the same 4' width as the outside sheathing. So you'll have to trim off (and usually waste) some strips equal to the thickness of the wall. But the waste here is negligible.

Think of your framing lumber in the same way. Look at the joist-span tables in chapter 14. By reducing the addition's size by a few inches, could you use joists of smaller size? Could you, for example, use 2 x 8 joists instead of 2 x 10 joists? Remember that there are a great many joists, so such a size reduction could mean a lot of money saved. Often, the room size reduction necessary for this kind of cost reduction is so small, you won't even notice it. But you have to plan it before you begin your foundation.

KNOW HOW BIG A ROOM YOU NEED

You can judge the room sizes you need by the furniture they'll contain. Similar existing rooms in your own or someone else's house are one guide. Cardboard cutouts on your graph-paper floor plan are another—and they make experimenting possible. Make the cutouts graph-paper-scaled to the floor area each piece of furniture occupies. You can measure the actual furniture you already have or get the dimensions of furniture you'll buy. Mail order catalogs often contain dimensioned outlines of the furniture shown in them. Or ask for such dimensioned diagrams where you plan to buy new furniture for your addition.

On your graph-paper addition floor plan, outline the room doors and draw little arcs to show where they'll swing when they're open. Then you can place your little scaled cardboard furniture outlines in different positions in the various rooms to see where they can be placed without obstructing doors. Often this shows you that one or more of your planned rooms doesn't have to be quite as big as you thought it should be. All this, of course, is based on the premise that you'd like to keep the cost of your addi-

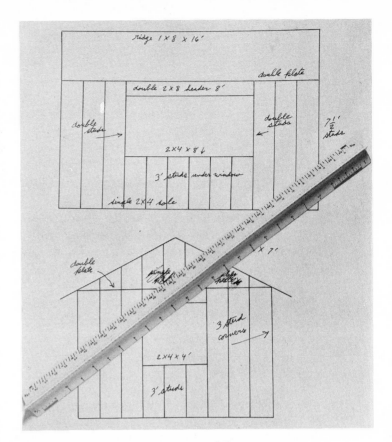

Fig. 30. Rough diagrams of your planned additions, like this, make it easy to figure lengths of framing lumber required. Triangular rule is scale rule, very helpful in this work. Use a plastic drawing triangle to square up corners.

tion as low as possible in keeping with the extra space it must provide. You don't have to cut everything to the bone. Where, for a feeling of luxury, or to carry out an idea, you want more space than you actually need, by all means plan it and build it. You only live once. But where you don't want it, stick to the necessary dimensions only. You may save for the extra space you need. If you start your planning well in advance of the actual work, you'll have the time to make revisions several times over. And the chances are that altogether new ideas will turn up. Greet them with an open mind. They may be better than your original plan. Sometimes it pays to take a new tack.

Fig. 31. To have a preview of your completed addition, take a snapshot of your house, have it enlarged (preferably to 8″ x 10″ size), then use tracing paper to sketch on addition. Photo enlargement need not be needle sharp to show overall effect.

A PREVIEW

If you'd like to know how your addition will look from the outside, there's an easy way to do it. Take a snapshot of your house as it is now, facing the wall that will be extended by the addition. For example, if your addition will be built on one end of the house, as viewed from the front, take your snapshot from the front, and have it enlarged—to 8″ x 10″ if your camera takes a sharp enough picture to allow that size enlargement.

Once you have your enlargement, lay a piece of tracing paper over it (art stores sell tracing paper in pads) and sketch in your addition. To get it to the right size, use something in the photograph as a ruler. For example, if you know that the front doorway is 3′ wide, you can use its width on the photo as a yardstick. If you want another scale, you can tape two pieces of paper to the house wall with their outer edges a measured distance apart—any distance you want—before you take the snapshot. They will then show in the picture and serve as a scale measurement for your

sketching. It's very simple. Houses are for the most part a matter of straight lines. So all you need to sketch your addition's outline is a ruler and a pencil. If you have artistic inclinations you can elaborate as much as you like. Shade the dark portions with a soft pencil to get a more realistic effect. Or, if you find you're fairly good at it, try color. You can make an overall tracing of the existing house and the addition, and color it much like a child's coloring book. If you've been thinking of changing the color of the house this can at least give you an idea of the different effects. All this is just the basic procedure. Expand it in any way you see fit to get the preview you want.

READY-MADE ADDITIONS

If you plan to add a ready-made addition, it's a simple matter to add it to your existing house floor plan, using graph paper as described earlier. There are several possibilities here. Cluster Shed

Add-A-Room modules are available ready for assembly in a variety of sizes. A greenhouse attached to your existing house is another possibility as an adjunct to a small living room. It can serve both for entertaining and for its designed purpose of growing plants. Lord & Burnham makes many types, ready for assembly. (You'll find the manufacturers' addresses in Appendix B at the end of this book.)

Fig. 32. Small greenhouse built on to living room or kitchen area can add interesting living area and provide year-round home-grown vegetables, flowers, or both. This one and two that follow are made by Lord & Burnham. Company offers many types for homeowner assembly. Note roll-down cover on top to provide sun shading in summer. LORD & BURNHAM

Fig. 33. To conserve heat greenhouses are available with double glass. This one provides plant-growing temperatures throughout winter in snow country. LORD & BURNHAM

Fig. 34. Interior view of full-height greenhouse that also serves as solar heating wall. Double glass and drapes may be used to conserve heat during nighttime hours. LORD & BURNHAM

Fig. 35. Light plus extra storage space by replacing an ordinary window with a bay window—a very low cost addition. Window seat has hinged lid for storage of blankets, bed linen and out-of-season clothes. Carpeted floor adds warmth. Carpet is product of Armstrong Cork Co., available in 12" x 12" self-stick squares, also in 12' wide roll form. ARMSTRONG CORK CO.

EXTRA SPACE AND STORAGE

In planning your addition, be sure to give some thought to bay windows and bow windows as a means of adding a little space and a lot of storage to a new room. While they cost more than ordinary windows of the same area, they can provide a window seat with storage space under a hinged top. You'll have to add this part yourself, but you'll have time to do it after the window's in place. If you're short of storage space, this can supplement your closets, old and new.

THE SHAPE OF ADDITIONS TO COME

Use the multiple-addition drawing to help in deciding where and how to build your addition. In some cases, more than one addition is the best answer. You might add a bedroom on one side of the house and a den on the other, or perhaps in back. The type of roof, too, depends on the individual situation. In general, a shed roof is easier and more economical to build than a gabled roof. If it's in keeping with the style of the house, it may be your best choice. Use the photo method described earlier to see how it would look where you plan to put it. You can have a conventional horizontal ceiling under a shed roof just as you can under a gabled roof. You'll find shed roofs on added wings of many picturesque old houses built in past centuries. They made the job of adding needed space easier and more economical, just as they do now. If they have a moderate pitch they can be shingled like a gabled roof. If they have a low pitch they can have roll roofing in a matched or blending color. As they are not a continuation of the original gabled roof, a shingle color match isn't essential. Where the low pitch keeps the roof surface from being seen from the ground (often the case), a smooth-surface roll roofing may be used on it and coated later with aluminum asphalt roof paint. This keeps the roof as much as 15 degrees cooler in summer. Something to think about if the room below it is to be air conditioned.

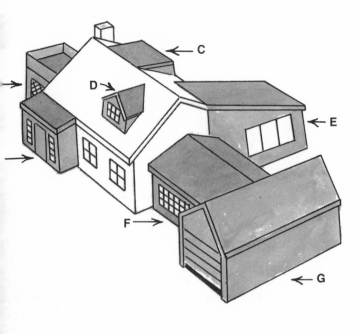

Fig. 36. Possible additions to an average house. (A) Vestibule extending from front door can be as shallow as 3', yet provide a coat closet and other conveniences. Example is shown in Fig. 40. (B) Ground floor room with low pitch shed roof may have deck on top, accessible through attic door. (C) Shed-type dormer can add full headroom space and light to attic. Framing is shown in chapter 16. (D) Gabled dormer is not as simple to build but can also add living space and light. It may conform better to the style of some houses. (E) Shed-roofed wing added to gabled roof, as shown, may actually improve appearance of house. One of the simplest ways to add sizeable living area. (F) Enclosed breezeway. If unattached garage is to be built or is already built close to house, enclosed breezeway provides sheltered access to it and adds living area, often family room. (G) Garage can be built from scratch or assembled from pre-fab components available from many lumberyards. If enclosed breezeway is planned, decide on garage type beforehand.

Fig. 37. Before the addition of a family room and new master bedroom, this Tudor style home might seem a problem for matching add-on. MASONITE CORP.

Fig. 38. Modern panel-type siding made this perfectly matched addition a simple job. Masonite brand "Stuccato" panel siding was used to match the original higher-priced stucco. MASONITE CORP.

Fig. 39. If, to match a traditional house, your addition must be faced with brick, there's no need for bricklaying if you use this panel-type brick siding. The material shown here is Marlite's Roxite man-made masonry paneling. It's available in blends of buff, red and white. Crushed stone surface is reinforced with fiberglass. Panels are $10^1/_4$" high, $48^1/_4$" long (horizontal) and are mounted with nails. MASONITE CORP.

Fig. 40. Vestibule built on to front entrance of early American house is entirely of plywood, painted to match shingles. It extends outward 3', has a stud at each corner plus one at the midpoint of each side. Door is at center, 32" wide, with stationary windows to match on each side. Some dealers call them all French doors, others call them casement doors. Explain clearly what you want if you plan similar vestibule, and expect to wait a day or so after ordering.

Fig. 41. Adding space upward. Unfinished shingles and under-height chimney show what was done. Originally, roof at right was lower than roof at left, now it's higher, adding bedrooms above living room in popular house design.

Fig. 42. Upward addition completed, chimney extended. House now has two more large bedrooms. Note storage shed to rear of house, at right.

ABOUT HEATING ADDITIONS

As a part of your overall planning, ask your heating contractor about extending your present heating system into the addition. Often this is the least expensive way to do the job, especially if you use maximum insulation in the addition—which you should do for today's obvious reasons. If your present heating unit can't handle the extra load, you have a choice of replacing it with a larger unit or using auxiliary heat in the addition. Electric heat is the easiest and usually the least expensive to add in this situation, but the cost of operation is higher than that of oil or gas in most instances. Check on both installation and operating costs before you decide on auxiliary heat or a larger heating unit. Get several estimates on each before you make up your mind.

Fig. 43. If original heating system leaves added living area too cool on exceptionally cold nights, Franklin stove or other wood stove may be most economical solution.

WINDOWS AND DOORS

The size and type of the windows in your addition can have a major effect on the overall appearance outside and general atmosphere inside. If the addition lengthens the main body of the house, the use of the same type and size windows as in the original house can sometimes create an effect that has been described as a parked train. The lengthened house simply looks too long. The use of a different window type in the addition can often eliminate this problem. You can head off such problems in most cases by using the photo-sketch procedure described earlier.

To know what types and sizes of windows are available, and at what prices, visit your local lumberyard—or several lumberyards, if you don't find what you want at the first one. During your visit you can look at booklets of window types and sizes and, in most instances, see an example of the actual window you select, before you buy it. For heating economy you'll be wise to use windows with double panes, like Thermopane. If you can't get the style you want with this type of glass, be sure to buy storm windows for the style you'll use.

Skylights

Where a chimney wall or other factors prevent you from having windows where you'd like them for ample room lighting, think about skylights. These are available from lumberyards in a variety of sizes,

Fig. 44. Bow window like this is ready-made item available from lumberyards. Diamond pattern grids are removable from inside to make window cleaning easier (on single large pane of glass). If you need storage space, add it under the window.

Fig. 45. Inside, bow window provides wide sill area for planters and ornaments.

though you may have to order the particular size you need. Made of glass or plastic (which can be double for added insulation), they're tough. Check on the price before you order, as they're not in the low price range. But they can often transform a gloomy room into a cheery one.

STAIRS

If your addition requires a stairway, you can save time (and often money) by having it built by a stair builder. Many professional home builders do. The stair builder needs to know the height of the stairs from floor to floor, the "run" of the stairs horizontally, and the width. He'll also want to know whether there will be a wall on both sides or one side. Typically, you can have your stairs ready to install in a few days. Be sure to get all details on price, type of wood (pine is cheaper than oak—when stairs won't have much traffic), extras like railings and delivery arrangements. The price may be lower than you expect.

Fig. 46. Easiest way to gain a family room in many modern homes is by adding carport like this one, next to existing garage, and converting garage to living area. Note garage door at right, before conversion.

Fig. 47. The final step, the following year, carport is enclosed to become new garage. Note picture window now in place of original old garage door. Family room is in area behind picture windows.

IV

Building the Foundation for Your Addition

11

HOW TO BUILD A FOUNDATION OR HAVE IT BUILT FOR YOU

Once you've decided to add to your house, the job begins with the foundation. Whether you build it yourself or have it built by a contractor often depends on the type and size of the foundation as much as on your budget. If the job is a big one you may not have the free time or the muscle to tackle it.

TYPES OF FOUNDATIONS

There are two general foundation types—the *pier foundation*, commonly used for porches and decks, and the *perimeter foundation*, usually used (and sometimes code-required) for added rooms. Most houses, too, are built on perimeter foundations.

The *pier foundation* consists of a number of separate posts (typically concrete), starting from underground concrete footings (bases) and extending upward to at least 8″ above the surface of the ground. If they are to support a deck only a foot or so above the ground, the masonry is usually extended up to the required height. If

Fig. 48. Lally column, left, supports girder. The Lally column is a concrete-filled steel pipe. Ready-made brackets attach it at upper end.

the deck is higher, wooden posts, Lally columns or poured columns are set on top of the masonry piers to serve as supports for the deck. Lally columns are steel pipes pre-filled with concrete. They're sold by lumberyards and building suppliers in various lengths. The pier foundation is inexpensive and a relatively easy do-it-yourself job. Digging the holes for the footings and piers is the only strenuous part. Concrete columns are sometimes poured in large fiber tubes called Sonotubes, available from building suppliers. (They are made by the Sonoco Products Company, Hartsville, S.C. 29550.)

The *perimeter foundation* is the continuous wall type. It, too, starts from underground footings and extends upward above ground as far as necessary to support the floor of the addition, as an added room. Because much more mason work is involved, however, the perimeter foundation is not as easy a do-it-yourself job as the pier type, though many are built by do-it-yourselfers.

Fig. 50. If you're building your own foundation of concrete block, specify the wall thickness, as blocks are made in several widths. These are 12-inchers at masonry yard. They're less expensive if you pick them up at the yard. But for a large job you'll do better having them delivered.

THINGS YOU SHOULD KNOW

About the Foundation's Depth

Whatever type of foundation you use, the footing from which it starts underground must be below the "frost line." This is the depth to which the ground can be expected to freeze during winter weather in the area. If the footing is above the frost line, the foundation may heave upward when the ground freezes and expands

Fig. 49. Sonotubes serve as the forms for pouring these concrete piers. After the concrete hardens, the Sonotubes are cut away with a trimming knife or other suitable tool.

under it, causing the whole structure above it to move. This can result in a variety of problems ranging from slanting decks to jammed doors and cracked walls. When you know the depth at which your foundation must start, you know how deep a trench must be dug (you can hire somebody to do this by machine) and how much mason work you'll have to do if you decide to do it yourself. (Complete details on how to do it follow shortly.) But before you decide, compare prices. Add up the cost of *all* the materials required to do it yourself, including concrete for the footings, blocks for the wall and mortar to hold the blocks together. If you feel the trench must be too deep to dig by hand, include the cost of having it dug by machine. You get prices on machine excavating by looking in the local phone book's Yellow Pages under "Excavating Contractors" or "Contractors—Excavating." The work is usually done by a machine called a backhoe and is priced by the hour for machine and operator. In asking for prices, be sure to tell the contractor where your house is located, as you'll usually have to pay for the time it takes to bring the machine to your location and take it back again. When you have your total, get estimates on having the whole job done by a contractor. Just open your phone book again to the Yellow Pages and look under "Foundations Contractors" or "Contractors—Foundations." You may find it costs little more to have the complete job done.

Matching Foundation Heights

More often than not, it's desirable to have the floor of the addition even with the floor of the room it adjoins. Usually this creates no problem, as the top of the exist-

ing foundation can be seen either from inside or outside. If, because of a finished interior wall and a greater-than-usual foundation overlap of siding on the outside, it's difficult to see the foundation top, you may have to make a small observation opening in the wall above the foundation. The best approach depends on the situation. Often you can pry out a shingle from the bottom course to get a view of the foundation top from the outside without disturbing the finished inside wall. Usually, you'll later remove shingles from the area where the addition joins the house anyway. It's important, however, to know the exact location of the existing foundation top before you start foundation work. This is true whether the floor of the addition is to be even with the floor of the room it adjoins, or a step above or below it.

Foundations for Irregular Terrain

Although most foundations are the same height all the way around, quite a few are not, as they are tailored to the terrain or the design of the structure they are to support. On sloping ground, for example, where a "walk-out" basement is possible, the foundation on the low side of the slope is often little more than a thick footing. This permits the installation of picture windows and sliding doors almost at ground level. (The bottoms of doors or picture windows should be just enough above ground level to prevent leakage from rain or melting snow.) The wall on the high side of the slope must, of course, be high enough to support the structure above ground level and provide adequate basement headroom.

In other instances, a low foundation is used under most of the building perimeter, with a wood framed wall extending up from it to floor level, while higher sections of foundation wall are used where required, as to support a masonry fireplace at floor level. Often, this type of height variation is essential to the appearance of an added room, as shown in the photos of the living room addition, chapter 25.

About Basements and Crawl Spaces

Unless you very definitely need extra basement space, don't build a basement (or have it built) under your addition. It greatly increases the cost of the job. The excavation must be deeper, drain tiles are usually needed around the footings, walls must be higher, and the basement needs a poured floor. Instead, build your foundation only as deep as required by the frost line—usually far less than basement depth. The space under the floor of the addition is then called a "crawl space." And it's important to dig off enough soil inside the perimeter foundation to actually permit crawling under the floor or walking, stooped over, to reach any plumbing or wiring that must be installed under the floor. It's also essential to provide some means of access to the crawl space in case repairs are necessary in the wiring or plumbing later on. If the new foundation is built on to a section of the original house wall that includes a cellar window, the window can provide access to the crawl space. If not, you can build a window into the foundation or provide a trapdoor in the floor. If there's no plumbing or wiring under the floor, it's still necessary (and very important) to provide air circulation in the space between the new floor and the earth. If you're having the foundation built for you, the contractor should know this. But make sure he does! Otherwise, the stagnant air and dampness invite wood rot in the floor framing. You can buy a wide variety of ready-made screened ventilators that can be installed in the foundation during construction. Select a type with down-slanted louvers to keep out rain, and favor a model that can be closed during extremely cold weather. One rule of thumb calls for ventilating openings having a clear area of not less than $\frac{1}{3}$ of 1 per cent of the enclosed area.

POURED CONCRETE FOUNDATIONS

Although you can build your own plywood forms, brace and join them, and pour your own solid concrete foundation, this type of job is best done by professionals for several reasons. For one, the chances are you won't save money by doing it yourself because you have to buy the materials for the forms and for the foundation. (Foundation contractors have ready-made forms that they reuse.) Another reason for having the work done by a contractor lies in the possibility of a homemade form giving way during the pouring process. If that should happen, you have a financial loss as well as the major problem of what to do with tons of concrete spilled where you don't want it.

In some cases, however, a do-it-yourself poured foundation is entirely feasible. If, for example, the foundation is to support a small structure like an added bathroom or a large floored bay window, it may be possible to pour the foundation without forms. Code permitting, you can simply dig a narrow trench to foundation depth where the foundation is to be. Then you simply have it filled with concrete from a mixer truck. It tends to level itself like pudding, though you'll usually have to work it a bit with hoe and trowel for final leveling. And you'll need your mason's level to make sure. It's a simple matter to build up a course or two of block on top of the poured foundation. The result, of course, is a combination wall that is its own footing. For this reason, check your local code before planning it.

Air-entrained Concrete

This is available from the usual suppliers if you ask for it, and has many advantages. Containing millions of tiny chemically created bubbles, it has a greater workability and durability. For exposed flatwork like sidewalks and terraces, it also has greater resistance to severe frost action and to the effects of salt for snow and ice removal. Where winter freeze-thaw conditions are likely, air-entrained concrete is definitely advisable. Ask your contractor or supplier about it. Many masons recommend it for all concrete work regardless of exposure.

About the Temperature

Foundations can be poured in winter, but it's best to leave the job to a contractor. The chemical used to prevent mixer-truck concrete from freezing before it hardens must be added in correct amounts by the supplier. Preparations should also be made in advance to protect the concrete. A thick blanket of straw without artificial heat is often protection enough for slabs on the ground. In other instances, however, housings or tarpaulins on wood frames must be used with a suitable source of heat. And precautions must be taken to keep the heat source away from flammable materials. Contractors have the required equipment and are experienced in its use.

HOW TO HAVE THE FOUNDATION BUILT FOR YOU

When you ask for estimates on having your foundation built, you'll probably reach some contractors who do the job with masonry blocks built up from a poured concrete footing and others who use poured concrete all the way—for both the footings and the walls. (The walls are poured in wooden forms that are removed after the concrete hardens.) Both methods are widely used and thoroughly proven. And you can get an advance estimate on the cost of either one, often over the phone. You must, of course, specify all dimensions. If your house is on steeply sloping terrain, it's wise to mention it, as the contractor may want to look it over before estimating. Experienced mason contractors who use block usually can make a firm estimate based on the foundation dimensions. Pricing of poured foundations is usually based on the number of cubic yards of concrete required. Typically, the concrete is charged directly to you by the supplier, who brings it in mixer trucks as it is needed by the contractor. You pay the contractor separately for his work according to his rate per cubic yard of concrete used in the foundation. Some contractors also work on an overall job price. Either way, be sure to get a *written* estimate covering the entire job. If you're not familiar with the contractor's reputation, check with your local Chamber of Commerce before you hire him. It's also a good idea at the estimating stage to ask him about other jobs he has done in the vicinity. If he does good work, he'll be glad to brag a little about specific examples. If timing is important to you, ask about that too. If there are no unusual problems, a fair-sized foundation can sometimes be completed in as little as one day. Naturally, however, you'll have to wait for it to harden before you can start building on it.

12

HOW TO BUILD
A PIER FOUNDATION

If you're building your own pier-type foundation for a deck or porch, check your local building code on the required size of the footings for the piers. It's the square horizontal area of the bottom and the thickness that count. In general, the heavier the load, the greater the footing area and thickness. If there's no code in the locality to provide specifics about footings, you can figure on 12″-square footings 8″ thick as a minimum for relatively small porches and decks. To be on the safe side, spacing between them shouldn't be more than 7′. For big decks where a large number of people are likely to congregate for parties and cookouts, use concrete footings about 20″ square and 10″ or 12″ thick, and limit the spacing to 6′. The same applies to a deck or porch that you plan to enclose later, as the larger footings will be necessary to handle the additional weight of the structure. Don't be surprised if you see decks with smaller footings and wider spacing. There are quite a few. But the cost of the footings (and the posts that go with them) is a very small fraction of the total cost of a deck, yet they are of prime importance. If you don't skimp you won't have to worry about puny little footings settling and sinking if your deck is later enclosed to become a music room with a grand piano in it.

HOW TO BEGIN

The first step in building a pier foundation is setting the locations of the piers to suit the size and location of the deck or porch you've decided on. Begin by marking the ends of the space along the wall where the deck will join the house. Then measure outward at right angles to the wall to the points where the corner post footings will be placed. There are various ways of making sure your outward measurements are at right angles to the house wall. One of the simplest, if you'll be using plywood, consists of using a standard 4′ x 8′ panel of it as a square. Set one 4′ edge firmly against the house foundation, at one of the deck-end marks along it, and the adjoining 8′ panel edge will be at right angles to the wall. Push a pointed dowel or metal rod into the ground next to the 8′ panel edge at the corner where it abuts the foundation, and tie the end of a ball of string to the rod or dowel. It's then a simple matter to draw the string taut in line with the 8' panel edge. You can then unwind more string, keeping it taut and in line with the panel edge until the string extends a little beyond the point where the corner footing will be. (You can mark this point approximately, in advance, using a steel tape rule of sufficient length.) Then push another dowel or rod into the ground and tie the string to it, keeping it taut. It's then a simple matter to use the steel tape rule to measure accurately from the wall outward along the string to the center of the corner footing to come. Drive a rod or stake at that point. Repeat the procedure to locate the other corner footing. You then have the rectangular outline of your deck or porch—two inner corners along the house wall and two outer corners marked by stakes or rods at a measured distance out along the string. Double check for squareness by measuring the diagonals between inner and outer corners. If the diagonals are equal, everything is properly squared. If they're not equal, recheck your measurements and adjust the outer corner rods as needed to square up. Then tie another taut string between these outer corner rods. The intermediate footings along the outer edge of the deck will be located along the line formed by the string. Measure their spacing and drive a rod next to the string at the points where the center of each footing will be located.

DIGGING AND THE CONCRETE WORK

If you're an average homeowner you probably already have most of the tools you need for the digging and concrete work. You'll need a pointed shovel, a spade, a hoe and a wheelbarrow (or garden cart). The wheelbarrow is used first in moving the portland cement, sand and crushed stone to the working area, then as a trough for mixing the concrete. You'll also need a hammer and a saw for making the forms for your piers, if they're to be poured.

Begin the digging by cutting a square outline of footing size around each of the rod-marked footing locations. These outlines should have their inner and outer sides parallel to the house wall. You can remove the sod from each outlined square with the spade. Then use the pointed shovel (because it makes digging easier) to dig the holes to the required depth *slightly* smaller than the outlines. If you're in an area where the ground doesn't freeze in winter, you need only dig off the soft topsoil far enough to provide a firm base. You square up the hole to full size with the spade, which has a blade better suited to making flat-sided and squared cuts. The hoe may come in handy for removing loose soil from the bottoms of deep holes and leveling the bottoms.

YOUR CHOICE OF PIERS

Once the holes are dug, you have a choice of footing and pier combinations. If the footings are to be only around a foot square and a foot or so deep, the simplest way to complete the job is by placing a square wood form 6" to 8" high around the top of the hole and filling the whole thing with concrete. If wood posts are to be mounted on top of the concrete, you place a wood batten across the top of the wood form with a ½" bolt suspended in it, head down with a washer. This provides a means of anchoring the wood post to the masonry. To keep rain from puddling on top of the concrete pier (which can rot the base of the wood post), you can trowel a little extra concrete on the pier top to provide a down-slope from the post outward to the edges of the pier.

If the footing must be deeper in the ground to get below a frost line, you can pour the footing to the required thickness in the bottom of the hole, typically about 8″ thick for small footings, 10″ to 12″ for larger ones. Then you can build up to 6″ or 8″ above ground level with masonry blocks cemented together. This is sometimes easier and less expensive than making the entire pier of solid concrete, and the masonry above the footing can be smaller than the footing. The masonry blocks are cemented one on top of the other with cement mortar.

POURED CONCRETE PIERS

You can also build a poured cylindrical concrete column from the footing upward to a few inches above ground level or all the way to the deck using the Sonotubes described earlier. You can cut these to the required length with a wood saw. You simply stand them on top of the hardened footing, pack a little earth around the base to keep the concrete from seeping out and fill the tube to the top with concrete. If the tubes must be too high to hold firm this way, you can brace them. Bolts can be embedded in the top, as described earlier, if needed. If the poured posts are tall, a reinforcing rod (or rods) should be set inside before the concrete is poured. For light porches and decks the Sonotube may be used to pour the entire footing and pier. Just select a diameter with enough cross-sectional area, dig a hole for it, and fill it with concrete, providing anchor bolts if needed. After the concrete sets, cut away the fiber tube above ground level. That portion below ground level gradually disintegrates.

Fig. 51. Footing is poured concrete between wood forms. Here, vertical rods have been pushed into ground below footing and marked for footing depth. They are removed after pouring, while concrete is still soft.

13

HOW TO BUILD
A PERIMETER FOUNDATION

The first step in a perimeter foundation is laying out the outline, in the same general manner as for the pier locations previously described. But instead of digging a number of individual holes, you must dig a continuous trench to the required depth, wide enough to take the forms for the footings and allow working space for the foundation wall construction. In general, the trench should be several feet wider than the footings. The footing width and wall thickness are usually specified by the local code. If there's no local code, the usual rule of thumb in normal soil calls for making the footings as deep (vertical thickness) as the thickness of the wall to be built, and twice as wide as the wall thickness. Thus, if your wall is to be 8″ thick (common in masonry block work), your footings should be 8″ deep, from top surface to bottom surface, and 16″ wide. The forms in which they are poured can be made of nominal 2 x 8 lumber with a nominal 1 x 2 nailed along one edge. As the nominal 2 x 8 lumber is actually only 7¼″ wide, the 1 x 2 (actually ¾″ thick) brings the overall width up to 8″. The forms are staked in place as shown in Fig. 51. It is very important that the forms

be level in the bottom of the trench. You can check this as you work, using a long level, preferably a mason's level. If one end of any section of lumber is too high, dig out enough earth under it to level it. If an end is too low, lift it as necessary and pack some soil under it firmly to prevent the concrete from flowing out during the pouring.

As much more concrete is required for a perimeter footing than for pier footings, you can either rent a cement mixer (from a tool rental service like United Rent-Alls) to mix it, or order it delivered by ready-mix truck. If you mix your own, for fairly heavy footings where maximum strength and waterproofness are not required, you can use a mix of 1 part portland cement to 3 parts sand and 4 parts crushed stone. If you want maximum strength and waterproofness as for a driveway, a good mix consists of 1 part portland cement to 2¼ parts sand and 3 parts crushed stone. This costs more, as it contains a higher proportion of cement. For work like footings, you can use about 6¼ gallons of water for each cubic foot bag of cement if the sand is just damp, as it normally is from outside storage. If it's wet, use only about 5½ gallons, and if it's very wet, reduce the water to about 4¾ gallons. If you order it delivered by ready-mix truck, just tell your supplier what you want it for, and he'll know the mix you need. Either way, allow about 5 to 10 per cent for waste. *Important:* Take advantage of your supplier's knowledge and experience whenever you can. He can offer advice on many aspects of the work (especially as applied to the particular locality). But—he's not likely to do so unless you ask questions.

Mixer truck concrete, of course, makes the job much easier. The truck has a metal chute that can be extended with lock-on sections to reach a considerable distance. But ask about its reaching range before you order. You'll need to pour your footing at a number of points along its perimeter, and you may want to make plywood chutes if the truck's chute can't reach all the necessary points. You can also use a wheelbarrow to carry some of the concrete to hard-to-reach spots.

Assuming your wooden forms are level, they serve as "screed boards." This simply means that after you've filled the space between them with concrete, you can place a short board across the form boards and slide it along to smooth off the concrete. This works best if you shimmy the board back and forth with a sort of sawing action as you go. If any hollows appear in the concrete surface, fill them in with a little extra concrete, and screed the area smooth. This procedure gives you a flat and level surface automatically if the wooden form boards are leveled in advance.

GIRDER FOOTINGS

Although the outer foundation walls

support much of the weight of the wood-framed structure above them, a beam called a girder, usually about midway between the front and rear walls, supports an even greater load than either of the walls. This beam is supported at the ends in pockets in the end walls or by masonry posts built up from the end wall footings. In between the end walls it is supported by posts that rest on individual square concrete footings. The posts are most often Lally columns (described earlier) which are available in a variety of lengths from building suppliers. The girder itself is most often made up of several pieces of stock-sized lumber nailed together. Typically, it might consist of three pieces of nominal 2 x 10 lumber. (It's much easier to lift 2 x 10 lumber into position and nail the pieces to-

Fig. 52. Here at left, vertical column of 12" block in wall of 8" block forms a pilaster on which girder is supported. Half blocks are used in wall to provide straight vertical joint at pilaster.

gether than to lift a solid 6 x 10 into place.) The end-to-end joints are arranged so as to come above the posts, and are staggered so that not all end-to-end joints occur over a single post. The girder makes it possible to use smaller joist (floor beam) sizes, without a sagging or springy floor, by reducing the span of the joists between supports. The girder top must be even with the wooden sills atop the foundation walls. More information about this is contained in chapter 14. Your local building code will usually specify the lumber sizes for girders and joists for different spans. But that comes later. When you build your foundation, however, you must also provide the footings for the posts that will support the girder. These must be of the size specified in your local code but, lacking a code, not less than 20″ square by 12″ thick and not more than 7′ apart, for an addition of average structural weight. The girder takes *twice* the load of the outer walls—so don't stint on the girder footings or the girder.

After the wall and girder footings have set up hard—at least overnight, depending on the weather—you're ready to start building the foundation walls. On a do-it-yourself basis, this is usually done with masonry blocks.

One of the most commonly used block sizes is nominally 8″ x 8″ x 16″, though it's actually 7⅝″ x 7⅝″ x 15⅝″ in order to allow for a ⅜″ thick mortar joint. The blocks are laid in a staggered, overlapping pattern like bricks. Where a wall starts from an existing wall of the house, half blocks are used in alternate courses, as shown, to start the overlapped pattern. Where the new wall abuts the existing house wall, it's important to scrub the old wall clean of soil to assure a good cement bond between the old and the new.

THE FIRST COURSE

You begin by laying a row (called a course) of blocks on top of the footing, starting from the existing wall. It's wise to do this "dry" before you mix or use any mortar. This way, you can space the blocks as they will be in the finished job and cut blocks if necessary to come out even at the end of the wall. If possible, however, plan your walls to avoid block cutting. (More about how you cut the blocks later.) As the blocks are "nominally" 16″ long, allowing for mortar, three of them add up to 4′, making it easy to match the foundation dimensions to the walls of 4′-wide plywood or other panels likely to be used in the room walls supported by the foundation.

To Keep It Straight

Use a taut string at right angles to the house wall, as described earlier for piers, to get the blocks in a straight line, and use a large square, like a framing square, to square the corners. Be sure, too, that the blocks are placed in the center of the footings. If the footings are properly squared, there should be no complications. Allow ⅜″ space between the block ends, and mark their positions wth pencil marks along the top of the footings. Carry the pencil marks out well beyond the position of the blocks so the mortar to be used later won't cover the marks. (Professional masons don't do this, but it's a wise procedure for non-pros.)

THE MORTAR

For most masonry block work a mortar made up of 2 parts masonry cement and 4 to 6 parts mortar sand does a good job. The masonry cement mentioned consists of part portland cement and part hydrated lime. The lime makes it stick better on surfaces where it might slide off while still wet. If you buy your mortar pre-mixed dry in bags, the instructions will tell you how much water to add. If you make your own, mix the cement and sand thoroughly "dry" and then add water until the consistency of the mix is right for applying to the blocks. You want it to stick to the vertical end surfaces of the block without slipping off and you want it soft enough for easy spreading with a trowel. Your best bet is a small trial batch. See how well you can make it stick to vertical surfaces of a block. If it's too stiff, use a little more water in your next batch to make it softer. If it's too slushy, use less water. You're not likely to have a problem here if you add the water in *small* amounts until the consistency looks right. Adding too much water to a mix that's a little too stiff can suddenly make it slushy. Use your small batch to get the knack. As the sand is usually stored in the open, it may be damp or wet, depending on the weather. If the sand is wet, of course, less water is required to bring the mix to the proper consistency.

LAYING THE BLOCKS

Start by spreading a bed of mortar about $3/8''$ thick on top of the footing where the first block will be placed, abutting the existing house foundation wall. Be sure the house foundation wall has been scrubbed clean of soil as mentioned earlier. Butter the end of the block that joins the house foundation with mortar to bond it to the house foundation. Then set the block in

the previously spread bed of mortar and push it against the house foundation to make a $3/8''$ mortar joint. To continue the course of block, simply repeat the process. You can butter the joining end of each block as you lay it in its bed of mortar, or you can butter the end of the block already laid, or do a little of each. Pick the method that you like best. But maintain the $3/8''$ mortar joint as well as you can. When you reach the corner of the footing, butt the end of one block against the side of the one it joins at right angles, as in the diagram, after buttering the joint with mortar. Keep track of the pencil marks you made when you laid the blocks "dry" to make sure the blocks will be spaced correctly to fit at footing corners and where they abut the existing house wall. Use taut string, as shown, to be sure the course of blocks is straight. And use a level to make sure the blocks are level. You can adjust off-level blocks easily by lifting the low end and working extra mortar under it. Or if the mortar is too thick under the high end, try working that end down to squeeze out a little mortar.

Generally, after the first course of blocks is completed, the outer corners are built up to the final height of the wall, as shown in the photo, to serve as a guide in building the rest of the wall plumb and to the correct height. The sections of the wall between the built-up corners can then be filled in easily, as the first course of blocks has already established the proper spacing.

FROM THE FIRST COURSE UPWARD

In laying successive courses above the first one, you spread the mortar on top of the block already laid, then place the upper block on it, after buttering the new

Fig. 53. *After single course of block is laid and cemented, foundation is built up at corners, like this, to provide vertical guide for remainder of wall. Note cement mortar on edges of first course of block, ready for second course.*

block end with mortar for the usual ³/₈″ joint with the preceding block. Usually, the mortar between courses is spread only along the long edges of the previously laid course of block, that is, the edges that will be the inside and outside of the wall. Where the new foundation abuts the original house foundation wall, half blocks and whole blocks in alternate courses make the staggered block pattern come out even. The corners, as shown in the photographs, work out automatically in finger joint fashion. Use the plumb vial of the mason's level to make sure the wall is plumb as you work. Use the level also to be sure each block is level. In all block work keep an eye on the spacing of the blocks as you work. If you find the blocks are staggered unevenly at some point along a course, you can bring the spacing back to normal by a slight adjustment in the mortar joint thickness between blocks. But the sooner you notice the problem, the easier it is to correct it, as

Fig. 54. *Second course of block is cemented to first course between corners, during overall buildup of foundation wall.*

Fig. 55. *Wall in foreground is now two courses high, back wall complete. Note "buttering" of cement near corner. This smooths surface of exposed areas of wall, aids in sealing wall below grade.*

wide variations in mortar joint thickness should be avoided. Fortunately, if your spacing happens to get more than a little out of kilter (not likely if you watch it), you can still correct it by cutting a block. Just be sure to wear protective goggles when you do so.

You can cut a block by making a deep groove in the block sides with a hammer and brick chisel, then by tapping the chisel into the ends of the groove until the end of the block cracks off. This calls for some practice, but you can try it several times on a single spare block. An easier way, if you have a portable circular saw, calls for the use of a masonry blade in the saw. This is really a thin abrasive wheel that cuts

Fig. 56. When using any type chisel to shape or cut masonry, protect your eyes with goggles, as chips can be injurious. These goggles are made by Stanley. STANLEY TOOL CO.

Fig. 57. Brick set is broad chisel-like tool used for cutting brick and block. GOLDBLATT TOOLS

Fig. 58. Mason's hammer (also brick hammer) is another tool used for cutting brick and block. Same goggle rule applies. GOLDBLATT TOOLS

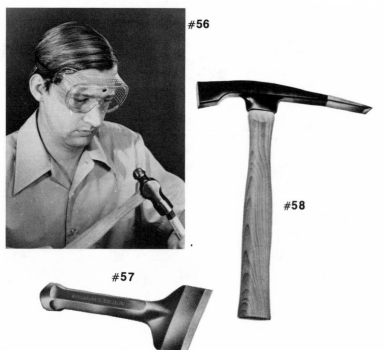

#56

#58

#57

through the block, but it must be used with care to avoid breaking the wheel. In *any* block cutting, wear protective goggles. (As with any type of work you haven't tried before, it's helpful, if you have the opportunity, to watch a professional do it before you try it yourself. If any masonry block work is in progress in your neighborhood, have a look at it for a while as it's being done.) The top course of the wall should be solid block, often 4″-thick solid blocks.

ANCHORING THE HOUSE TO THE FOUNDATION

Although it's not always done unless the local code requires it, you'll be wise to bolt the framework of your addition to the foundation, especially in high-wind localities. The usual procedure for locking bolts into the foundation calls for setting screening in the horizontal mortar joint (when it's made) two courses down from the top of the wall, at the location of the anchor bolts. If the foundation is to be capped with solid blocks, leave a gap in the capping for this procedure. A bag of packaged dry-mix concrete can then be mixed in batches to pour into the hollow block cores at these locations. The screen prevents the fresh concrete from falling down through the wall. Anchor bolts can then be embedded head-down, with washers next to the heads. Leave enough threaded length projecting upward for bolting through the sill. The gap in the solid block capping can be filled in around the bolt with more of the concrete. Another method: stuff wads of newspaper down into the hollow block cores where the bolts are to be located, and pour concrete on top of the newspaper. The paper serves the same purpose as the screen.

V

Building the Framework on a Perimeter Foundation

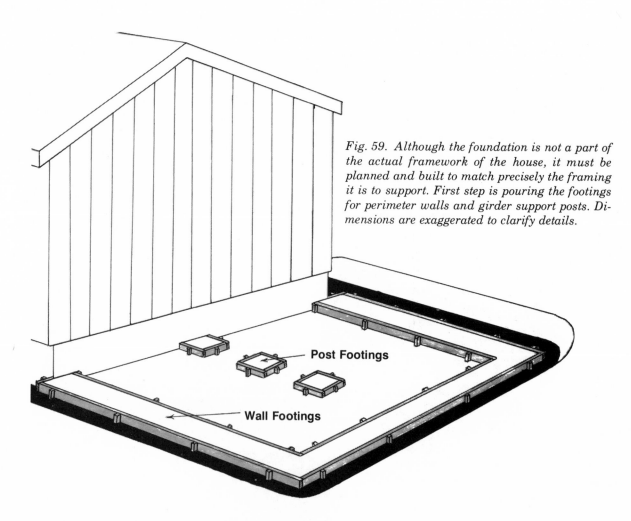

Fig. 59. Although the foundation is not a part of the actual framework of the house, it must be planned and built to match precisely the framing it is to support. First step is pouring the footings for perimeter walls and girder support posts. Dimensions are exaggerated to clarify details.

Post Footings

Wall Footings

14

STARTING THE FRAMEWORK
OF YOUR ADDITION

You can start building the framework of your addition as soon as the foundation is hard. You do the job the same way professionals do it, by following the simple rules that apply regardless of room size, within the usual residential dimensions. Whether you're building a small bedroom or a spacious living room, for example, the wall framing is basically similar, except for overall dimensions, and is made up mainly of nominal 2 x 4 lumber.

Floor and roof framing, too, follow largely standardized rules, but the cross-sectional dimensions of the lumber depend on the "span." You use heavier joists (floor beams) and rafters (roof beams) for wider spans between supports. Typically, the span of floor joists is the distance between the foundation wall that supports the outer joist ends and the "girder" that supports the inner ends.

The required cross-sectional sizes of joists and rafters for different spans are specified in most local building codes. If you're building in a locality where there is no code, you can obtain a copy of a code used in a nearby community or use the tables of sizes given shortly.

FRAMING METHODS

Although there are several methods of framing a house or an addition, the Western or platform frame shown in this chapter is one of the most widely used and probably the easiest for the do-it-yourself builder. In this method, the floor is framed and completely covered with subflooring to serve as a working platform before the wall framing begins. The perimeter frame in this type of construction is sometimes called a "box sill" because of its simple, box-like form.

EXAMINE A BUILDING JOB IF YOU CAN

If there's any home construction in progress in your area or within reasonable driving distance, take a look at it with special attention to the framing. If you can manage to do it on a day when the work is actually underway, you may also note a work-saving pointer or two of the professional's working techniques. But don't be surprised if the job you happen to see differs somewhat from the basic methods shown in this chapter. There are many acceptable variations in detail, some of which are illustrated later. And individual builders have their preferences. Local codes, too, often vary in their requirements from one area to another.

NOMINAL LUMBER SIZES

As the lumber used in home construction is sold in "nominal" sizes, it's important to familiarize yourself with the nominal dimensions, which are smaller than "full" size. Keep in mind, too, that these nominal sizes have been revised in recent years and are now generally a little smaller than they used to be. Essentially, the nominal size system in framing lumber sizes works like this: all nominal 2″ thick lumber is actually 1½″ thick. As to width, the actual dimension of lumber less than 8″ wide is ½″ narrower than the nominal dimension. Thus a nominal 2 x 4 is really 1½″ x 3½″. In widths of 8″ or more, the nominal width is ¾″ narrower than the stated dimensions. So a 2 x 8 is really 1½″ x 7¼″. A 2 x 12 is really 1½″ x 11¼″. Nominal 1″ thick lumber is actually ¾″ thick, but its widths follow the same rules as nominal 2″ lumber. The charts and tables of such things as joist and rafter sizes (given in this chapter and in many building codes) are based on nominal sizes, so they apply to lumber the way you buy it at the lumberyard. The length of lumber, however, is in full lengths. If you buy a 10′ piece of 2 x 10, it will be a full 10′ long. Plywood thickness too is the full dimension. When you buy ½″ plywood, it's ½″ thick. The reason for the differences between nominal and full size lumber lies in the shrinkage of the lumber during the drying process and in the material removed smoothing the lumber surfaces. It's full size when it comes from the saw, but it's considerably smaller when it's ready for use. And, as the greater shrinkage occurs across the grain, the wider the piece, the greater the proportional shrinkage. Lengthwise, however, shrinkage is minimal. So your lumber is full length for all practical purposes.

When your room reaches the finishing stage, you'll probably need moldings of various sizes and shapes, including baseboards, shoe moldings and other trim items. Your best bet, here, is a visit to the molding racks at your local lumberyard. When you see the moldings, you can select the ones you want without guesswork. You may also be using finishing grade lumber dimensioned by "quarters." One widely used size in this system is called ⁵⁄₄, but it's *not* 1¼″ thick. It's thickness is actually 1⁵⁄₃₂″. The system runs all the way to ¹⁶⁄₄ (actually 3¾″ thick).

The importance of knowing nominal sizes becomes apparent when you need to add up the overall thickness of structural components of a wall or floor. You must base your figuring on the nominal sizes. If you were to base it on full sizes, your total would be far "over."

THE CARPENTRY BEGINS WITH SILL AND GIRDER

As shown in the drawings, the framework of your addition starts with the wooden "sill" that's bolted to the top of the foundation wall. In the past, this was set in a creamy cement and water mixture called "grout," which is still used in many instances. The purpose of the grout is that of sealing the juncture between foundation

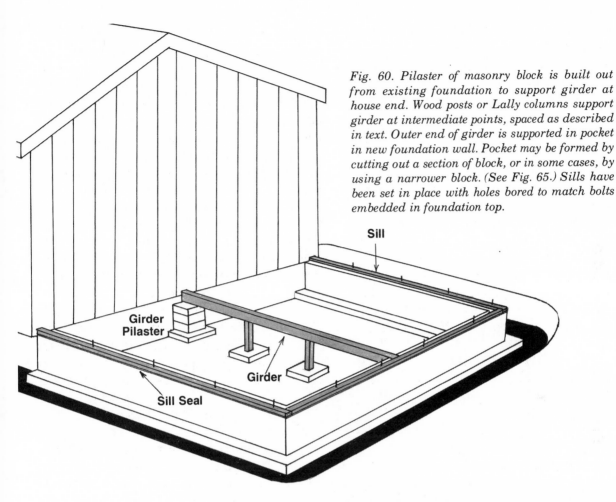

Fig. 60. Pilaster of masonry block is built out from existing foundation to support girder at house end. Wood posts or Lally columns support girder at intermediate points, spaced as described in text. Outer end of girder is supported in pocket in new foundation wall. Pocket may be formed by cutting out a section of block, or in some cases, by using a narrower block. (See Fig. 65.) Sills have been set in place with holes bored to match bolts embedded in foundation top.

Sill

Girder Pilaster

Girder

Sill Seal

Fig. 62. Light-colored material protruding just above foundation is fiberglass sill sealer.

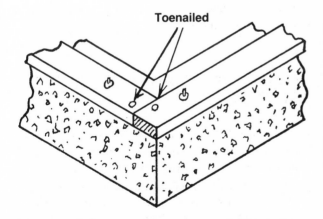

Toenailed

Fig. 61. Toenailing with 3" common nails is indicated (by open circle nail heads) for plate members at foundation corner.

Starting the Framework of Your Addition   77

and sill to keep out drafts when the building job is completed. Today, however, the juncture is often sealed with a narrow strip of soft, thin fiberglass made for the purpose and called a sill sealer. When the sill is tightened down, the fiberglass compresses into any irregularities, sealing the foundation-sill juncture. This method has the advantage of being usable even in very cold weather when grout might freeze before the sill could be tightened down.

THE GIRDER

The girder is the other part of your framework's base. It's a heavy beam that runs at right angles to the joists, usually near the center line of the building to provide support for the joists between foundation walls. Thus the "span" is cut in half, making the use of joists of much smaller cross section permissible. In some instances, for example, it might be feasible to use 2 x 6 joists with central girder support where it might be necessary to use 2 x 12 joists if there were no central support. The

table of span and joist sizes provides many other examples.

Typically, the girder is supported at its ends by "pockets" in the foundation masonry or by pilasters built out from the foundation walls. If it is supported in pockets, they must be large enough to allow air circulation to prevent dampness and rot. Between its ends, the girder is supported by posts, with their lower ends on concrete footings placed there for the purpose, as shown in the drawings. If a complete floor is to be laid (as in a basement), the post footings may be planned to provide a flush surface.

If there's no code in your area or if the code doesn't specify girder post spacing, it's wise to play safe by limiting the center-to-center spacing of the posts to a maximum of 7'. The reason for ample girder support lies in the important fact mentioned in the last chapter: the usual girder actually carries *twice* as much load as the foundation walls. The drawing of the three men carrying two heavy logs is an illustration explaining what happens. The man in the center (representing the girder) is supporting the inner ends of both logs, hence half

Fig. 63. Why the girder supports approximately twice as much load as the foundation walls. Men at left and right, comparable to foundation walls, each support only one *end of* one *black beam. Man in center, comparable to girder, supports one end of* both *black beams, hence twice the load supported by the outer men.*

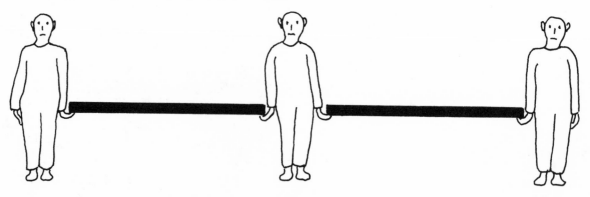

the weight of *both* logs. But the man at the outer end of each log (representing the foundation walls) supports half the weight of only *one* log. In a house structure the girder supports half the weight of the floor areas on *both* sides of it, while the foundation walls support half the weight of the floor area on only one side of the girder.

GIRDER SIZE

If your local code doesn't specify girder sizes, check on it with your building inspector. If there's no code, one rule of thumb often used is this: select your joist size first, following the span and size table in this chapter (or in the code of a nearby

Fig. 64. Three-piece girder is nailed together with 4″ nails, two near each end of both outer pieces, others staggered with a horizontal distance of 32″ between nails. If a four-piece girder is used, the additional part is nailed to the other three pieces with 4″ nails spaced in the same manner.

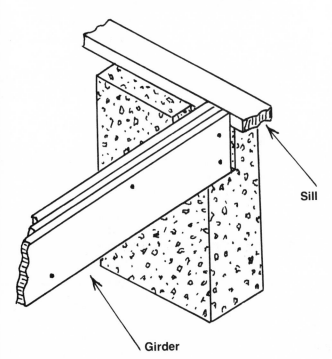

Sill

Girder

area). The span is figured from the inside edge of the sill to the nearest edge of the girder. Once you've selected the correct joist size for the span, build your girder from three layers of the same size lumber, nailed together. For example, if your joists will be of 2 x 10 size, your girder will consist of three 2 x 10's nailed together. As indicated in the nailing drawings and captions, you do the nailing with 4″ (twenty-penny) nails, two near each end of each piece, intermediate ones staggered with a horizontal distance of about 32″ between them. If there's any possibility of dampness in a masonry pocket that supports the girder, treat the girder end (or ends) with a rot-preventive preparation. (Steel beam girders are also sometimes used, though the cost is much higher and power equipment is necessary to install the steel beam.)

ALIGNING THE GIRDER

The top surface of the girder must, of course, be at the same height as the top surface of the sills so that the floor framing will be level and even. The easiest way to accomplish this is by installing the sills first, and tightening them down. The pockets or pilasters that support the girder should have their supporting surfaces slightly lower than the exact height required to bring the girder's top surface flush with the top surface of the sill. You can then use a scrap piece of girder-size lumber as a gauge in "shimming up" the supporting surfaces of the pockets or pilasters, as shown in Fig. 65. This is often done with concrete, which must be allowed to harden before the actual girder is set in place. This method enables you to bring

Fig. 65. Girder end in foundation wall pocket. Note that pocket has been made deeper (top to bottom) than girder dimension and "shimmed" up with wood block under girder. This is done so that girder top can be brought flush with top of sill on foundation simply by using shim block cut to required thickness.

the girder top flush with the top of the sill *after* the sill sealer is in place. As different brands of sill-sealing material compress to different thicknesses, it's not practical to plan on the exact height of the sill in advance.

JOIST SIZES

If there's no building code in your area, you can use the following table to select joist sizes for the span you'll use.

The sizes in the table are based on a live load of 40 pounds per square foot, a figure widely used for residential living areas. Note that the closer the joists are spaced, center to center, the greater the span allowed. The commonest spacing is

16", which is the spacing used in the additions shown in the photographs. You'll find some variations in tables like this from one code to another. Simply follow the one in your local code, if any. Otherwise use this one.

Nominal lumber size	Spacing of joists center to center (inches)	Maximum span (in feet)
2 x 6	12	9
	16	8' 6"
	24	7
2 x 8	12	12
	16	11' 4"
	24	9' 6"
2 x 10	12	15
	16	14
	24	12
2 x 12	12	18' 6"
	16	16' 6"
	24	14' 6"

Before the joists can be nailed in place, the sills and the girder must be measured and marked with a pencil for the joist locations. Note that, except for the outermost joists, the joist ends overlap at the girder. This overlap need not be any greater than the width of the girder, as greater overlap adds to costs without adding to strength. The outermost joists don't overlap. As they rest on the foundation-supported sill for their entire length, they are simply butted end to end where they meet. The butted joint is essential on the outermost joists to provide an even surface to which sheathing or siding can be nailed. A butt piece of joist-size lumber is sometimes nailed to the inside of the butt joint to keep it aligned until subflooring and sheathing are applied.

The usual method of assembling the

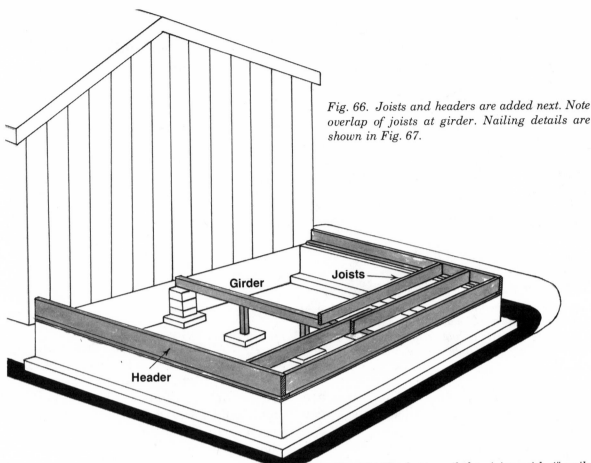

Fig. 66. Joists and headers are added next. Note overlap of joists at girder. Nailing details are shown in Fig. 67.

Fig. 67. Header is nailed to joists with 4" nails, three to end joist (at corner), two to others. End joist and header are toenailed to sill with 3" nails spaced 16" apart. If plywood sheathing is used in manner shown in Fig. 86, toenailing to sill is not necessary except to hold joist in place during construction.

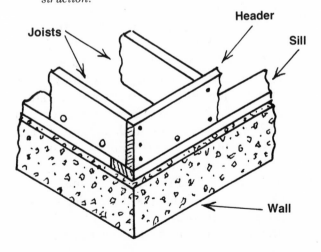

floor frame begins with the "headers" that are toenailed to the sills that run at right angles to the joist direction, and with the outermost (butted) joists. All of these are mounted atop the sill and flush with its outside edge. Once these members are nailed in place, they form a boxed-in rim around the perimeter of the foundation top. Intermediate joists can then be lowered into place between the headers. The outer ends of these joists are butted snugly against the headers and fastened by nails driven through the headers into the joist ends. At the inner ends (over the girder),

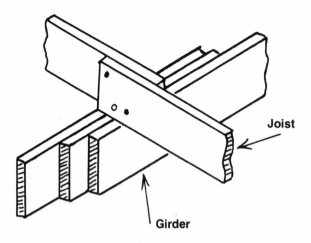

Joist

Girder

Fig. 68. Where joists overlap at girder, they are nailed together with two 3" nails and toenailed to the girder with one 3" nail on each side of the pair of joists. Here, toenailing is into center piece of girder. (Open circle indicates toenail.)

the overlapping ends of the joists are nailed together and toenailed to the girder as in Fig. 68.

When measuring inward toward the house from the outermost joist (to mark for intermediate joist spacing), measure first for the joist that will be farther from the outermost one at the overlap. This places the other overlapping joist closer to the outermost one, so that the spacing between them is a little less than the regular spacing. If the spacing works out so that the final overlapping joists nearest the house are farther from it than the regular spacing, add another pair of overlapping joists. Even if they result in closer-than-usual spacing, they assure a firm floor. A pair of end-butted joists are nailed through the house sheathing into the house framing to provide support for the subfloor at the juncture of the addition to the house. Generally, if the dimensions of the addition are planned in advance with panel materials dimensions and joist spacing in mind, no

extra joists with closer-than-usual spacing will be required.

FRAMING A STAIR OPENING

Where an opening through floor framing is required for stairs, joists are doubled on both sides of opening. Doubled headers are used at both ends of opening to support intermediate joist or joists. Doubled joists are nailed together like girder members.

ABOUT TRUSSES

If you want complete floor plan freedom, you can use trusses instead of joists. Like many highway bridges, these utilize a framework of diagonal braces between upper and lower members to achieve extremely high rigidity. (Figs. 71 and 72 show typical truss forms.) As a result, floor trusses can be used between foundation walls *without* a girder and its posts. This leaves your basement unobstructed and permits you to use it as one very large room or to divide it in any way you like.

If you use floor trusses, it's also logical to use roof trusses when you reach that stage. These give you the same wide span capabilities and floor plan freedom on your upper floors. As both floor and roof trusses must be built to match the house or addition dimensions, you order them through your lumberyard or building supplier. The drawings show the usual terminology. But as this varies to some extent in different areas, be absolutely sure that the basic dimensions are clearly understood when you order.

For residential use, most trusses are of wood, commonly with metal gussets hold-

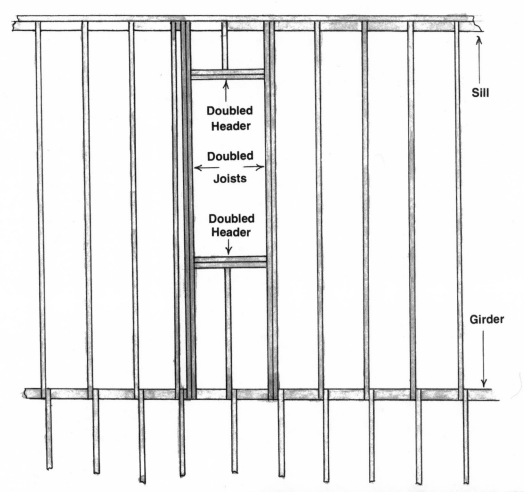

Doubled
Header

Doubled
Joists

Doubled
Header

Sill

Girder

Fig. 69. Framing a stair opening.

Fig. 70. Stairway made to order by stair builder awaits installation in house addition. Professional stair construction saves time, avoids errors. Details in text.

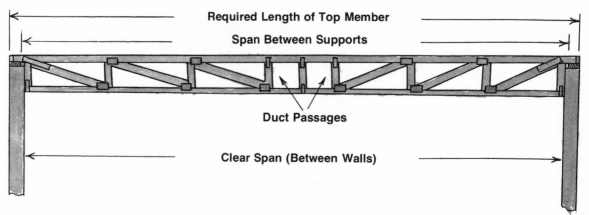

Required Length of Top Member

Span Between Supports

Duct Passages

Clear Span (Between Walls)

Fig. 71. Floor trusses, relatively new to residential construction, can eliminate the usual underfloor girder, leaving basement space clear and without posts. Duct passages can be provided for heat or air conditioning ducts, also plumbing and wiring. As some manufacturers use slightly different terminology, make certain all span dimensions are clearly understood when you order.

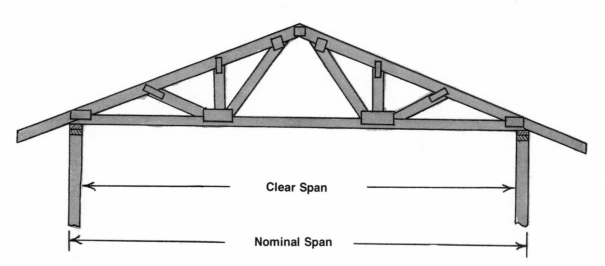

Clear Span

Nominal Span

Fig. 72. Roof trusses are available through building suppliers and lumberyards, ready-made to order, in sizes required. Clear span is usual term for span between insides of supporting walls. Nominal span is commonly span between outsides of supporting walls. Both are essential to assure proper seating of truss on plate. Make certain there is no misunderstanding of terms when you order.

ing the joints together, though some types of floor trusses are of metal. Space can be allowed for ducts and piping to pass through the trusses, as shown in the drawing.

If you plan to use trusses, gather specific data about the brand before you order. Your lumberyard or building supplier can usually provide much basic information in the form of folders or brochures. Ask about this in advance. And, of course, check with your local building department regarding any regulations pertaining to trusses.

THE SUBFLOOR

The subfloor, now usually plywood, is the layer of material applied directly over the floor frame of joists and headers. You nail it in place as soon as the floor frame is completed. A certain amount of power saw edge trimming is necessary (because of joist overlap) so that all plywood edges that run parallel to a joist will run along the center line of the joist. This way, the edge of the panel being nailed in place and the adjoining edge of the next panel can both be nailed to the same joist. The plywood panels should also be pencil-lined between edges for nailing to intermediate joists. This is easy to do merely by sliding the plywood so as to reveal the intermediate joists where they are visible first at one end of a plywood panel, then the other. Mark the joist center line locations at both ends of the panel, connect the marks with a pencil line along a straight edge, and when the panel is in final position, nail through the pencil line. When the floor frame is

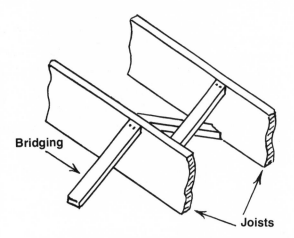

Fig. 73. Bridging pieces of 1 x 3 are nailed at each end with 2¹/₂" nails.

Fig. 74. Bridging. Criss-crossed bracing like this stiffens floor. Upper ends are nailed in place before subfloor is laid. Bottom ends may be nailed later. Lumber size used for bridging depends on code. Lacking code, nominal 1 x 3 is often used. If joist span is 10' or more, at least one row of bridging is needed (midpoint). In spans greater than 14' to 16' two rows are usually used, not more than 7' or 8' apart.

completely covered with plywood nailed in place, it becomes a very rigid platform. Typically, the plywood used with joists on 16″ centers is ½″ thick. If finish flooring (such as oak flooring strips) is to be nailed on top of the plywood, it is usually done after most of the work on the room has been completed. This reduces the chances of marring the finish flooring. If wall-to-wall carpeting is to be used, it can be laid directly on the subfloor or over a layer of underlayment or carpet cushion. Slightly thicker subflooring is often used, ⅝″ or ¾″ instead of ½″ thickness to assure a firm floor. It's also wise to nail short pieces of joist-size lumber between the joists under any subfloor seams that run *across* joists. These pieces provide support for the seams and also serve as nailing strips.

Fig. 75. Plywood subfloor is nailed with 2¹/₂″ nails not more than 6″ apart along edges of floor frame (as at header) and about 12″ apart along intermediate members (like joists). For maximum stiffness, surface grain of plywood should run at right angles to joists.

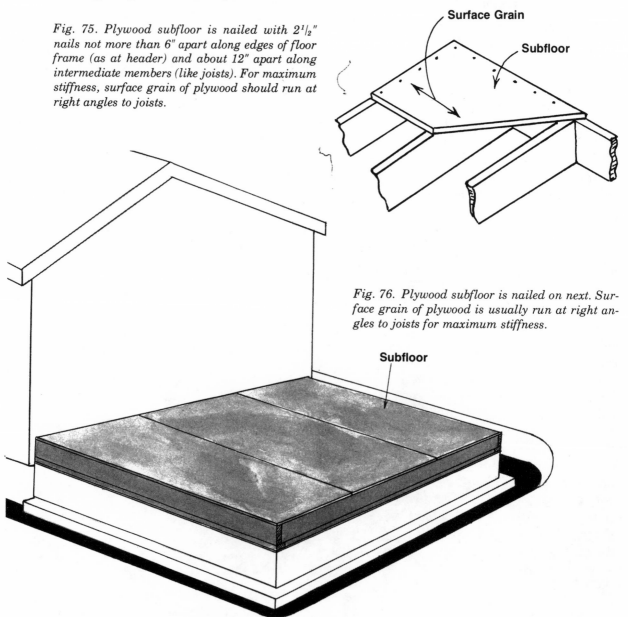

Fig. 76. Plywood subfloor is nailed on next. Surface grain of plywood is usually run at right angles to joists for maximum stiffness.

Subfloor

15

FRAMING WALLS AND CEILINGS

As soon as the platform floor is completed, the walls can be built. The building is usually done with the wall framing members laid out flat on the floor. The lower horizontal member of the wall frame is called the "sole" or sole plate, the upper one simply the plate. The vertical members between the two horizontals are called studs. These are fastened in place by 3½″ (16d, sixteen-penny) nails driven through the horizontals into the ends of the studs. If windows or doors are to be in any section of wall framing, openings for them are framed as shown in the detail drawings.

Some builders nail the plywood sheathing to the wall framework while it is still laid out flat on the floor. Others erect the framework and nail on the sheathing after that, while the wall frame is vertical. As the sheathed framework is considerably heavier than the framework alone, however, it requires a helper or two to stand it up. In any event, the wall should be braced by temporary diagonals as soon as it is erected. The diagonals may be removed as the work progresses, so as not to obstruct it. When all the walls are up, they tend to

brace each other. The walls are fastened to the floor and to each other at the corners, as shown in the nailing drawings.

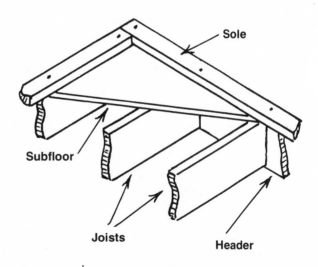

Fig. 77. Sole is nailed through subfloor into header and end joist with 3½″ nails staggered slightly, to avoid splitting header or end joist, and spaced 16″ apart.

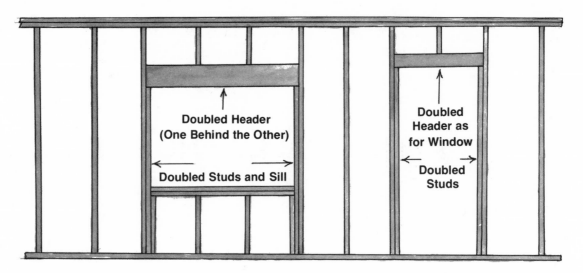

Doubled Header (One Behind the Other)

Doubled Header as for Window

Doubled Studs and Sill

Doubled Studs

Fig. 78. Wall framing goes up next. Usually it is nailed together laid out flat on floor, then tilted to vertical position and braced as shown in Fig. 82, after nailing through sole to floor. Some builders also nail sheathing to wall frame while it's flat on floor. Others erect framing, then nail sheathing to it. With sheathing on, wall is heavier, so you may need help to stand it up. Note how upper and lower plate members overlap at corners. Lower plate member is often omitted above header at wide openings. Header is then set against upper plate member. Do this where number of openings makes material savings substantial without excessive increase in working time. But check local code.

Fig. 79. Old-type wall framing. Doubled headers, one behind the other, above window and door openings, with wood spacers between header members to bring their outer surfaces flush with outer surface of wall framing. Short studs were set between top of header and bottom of plate. Doubled window sills (one above the other) were also common, frequently reinforced with short studs under them at ends. Stud spacing was usually 16″ on centers.

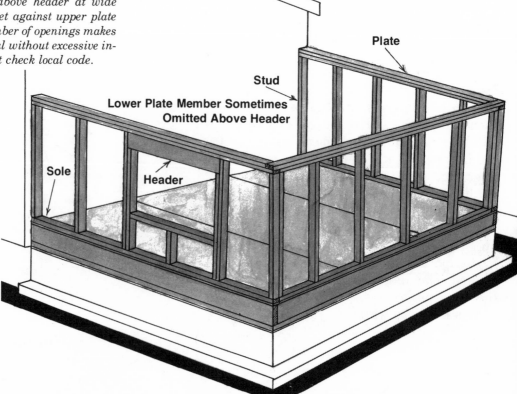

Plate

Stud

Lower Plate Member Sometimes Omitted Above Header

Sole

Header

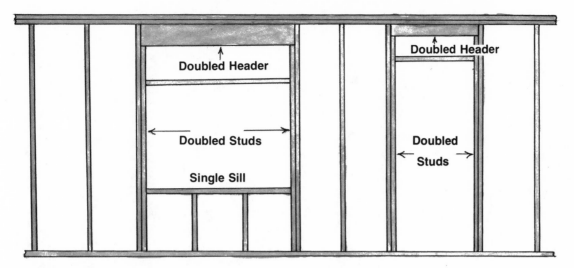

Fig. 80. *New-type framing has doubled headers above windows and doors located directly under plate, so no load reaches framing below it. Doubled headers are spaced flush with outer surfaces of wall frame, as usual. No short studs required above window. Sill is not doubled. Throughout the job, this method saves material, cuts costs, equals strength of older method.*

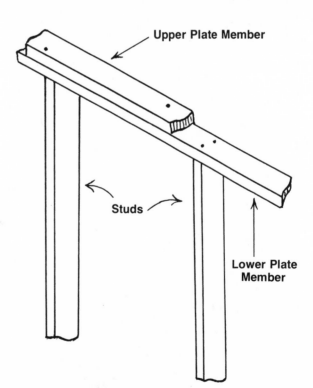

Fig. 81. *Lower plate member is nailed to each stud and corner post with two 3¹⁄₂" nails. Upper plate member is nailed to lower one with 3" nails staggered 16" apart. If wall frame is built laid out flat on floor, sole plate is nailed to studs in same manner as lower plate member.*

Framing Walls and Ceilings 89

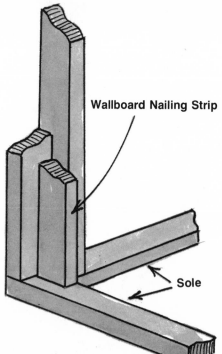

Wallboard Nailing Strip

Sole

Fig. 82. When erected wall must be left until next work day, it must be braced with temporary diagonal braces to floor, as shown. Both metal and wood braces are used here. Usually 2 x 4 braces are enough. Note section of wall framing lying on floor at extreme left, ready to be erected at next work session.

Fig. 83. How corner posts are assembled to provide nailing surface for both inside wallboard and outside sheathing. All members are 2 x 4 stock. Wallboard nailing strip is nailed to wall frame in foreground. Frames for both adjoining walls may be assembled in conventional manner.

SHEATHING METHODS

There are several ways of applying the plywood sheathing to the wall framework, as shown in the drawings. In one, the sheathing extends from the upper surface of the top plate to the bottom of the sole plate and no farther. In the other, the sheathing extends below the sole all the way down to the sill that rests on top of the foundation. Depending on the overall height of the wall, this may require the use of horizontal nailing strips between studs near the top of the wall frame to provide for wind tight nailing of an upper section of plywood to complete the wall. Extending the sheathing all the way down to the foundation sill, however, locks the framework of the house solidly to the foundation, and is therefore often done in earth tremor and hurricane areas. Naturally, because of the additional material used, it increases costs.

Fig. 85. Widely used method of applying sheathing to wall frame. Sheathing is cut flush with bottom surface of sole and top surface of plate. Sole is set inward from outer surface of subfloor by a distance equal to thickness of sheathing. So, sheathing is flush with outer edge of subfloor, also with outer surface of header or outer joist.

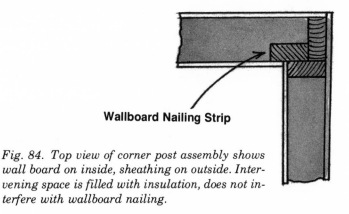

Wallboard Nailing Strip

Fig. 84. Top view of corner post assembly shows wall board on inside, sheathing on outside. Intervening space is filled with insulation, does not interfere with wallboard nailing.

Fig. 86. In areas where earth tremors or very high winds are likely, sheathing may be carried all the way down to upper surface of foundation and nailed to sill, header, sole, etc., locking entire assembly together. Sill on top of foundation must be set back from outer surface of foundation by distance equal to thickness of sheathing. For usual interior ceiling height, this may require an extra section of sheathing at top and a nailing strip, as shown, as 8' plywood panel may not be long enough, depending on joist dimensions. Half-inch plywood sheathing is nailed with $2\frac{1}{2}$" nails spaced 5" apart along panel edges, 10" apart along intermediate framing members.

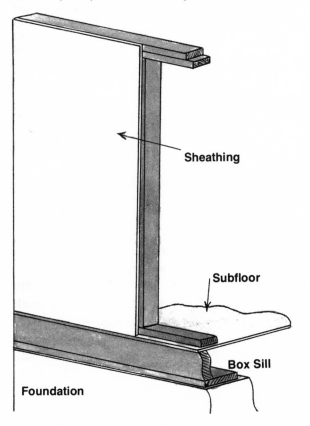

Sheathing

Subfloor

Box Sill

Foundation

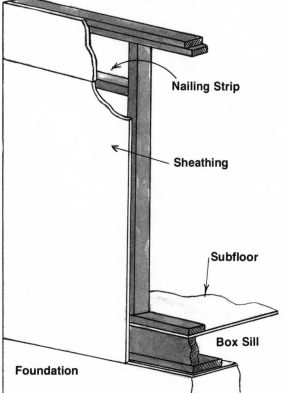

Nailing Strip

Sheathing

Subfloor

Box Sill

Foundation

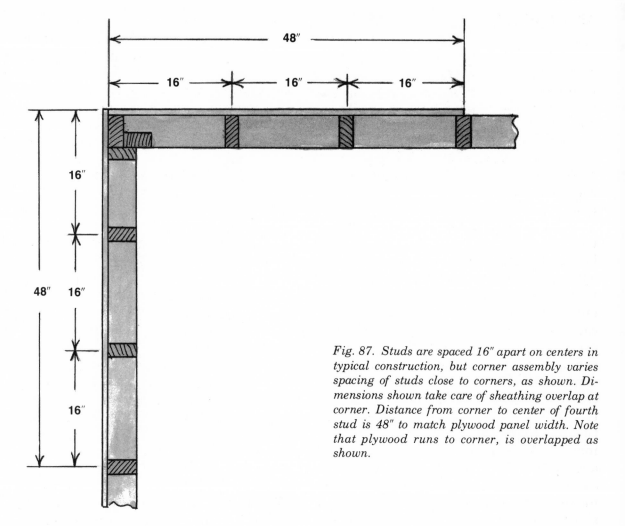

Fig. 87. Studs are spaced 16″ apart on centers in typical construction, but corner assembly varies spacing of studs close to corners, as shown. Dimensions shown take care of sheathing overlap at corner. Distance from corner to center of fourth stud is 48″ to match plywood panel width. Note that plywood runs to corner, is overlapped as shown.

LEAK SEAL

After the sheathing is applied, it's wise to apply a layer of 15 lb. asphalt felt (you may think of it as tarpaper) over the sheathing. This may be stapled on with a staple gun, starting at the sill on top of the foundation and working up to the top of the wall. The felt comes in rolls 3′ wide and is fastened in place in horizontal strips cut to wall length or shorter, for convenient handling. The seams should be overlapped about 2″ shingle fashion (upper strip overlapping lower strip) to shed any water outward from the sheathing.

The siding is applied next, and if it's properly applied, not much water is likely to leak through it. But the felt layer provides a safety barrier against dampness. Note: If you use vinyl siding, check the instructions. Some should be used without the felt.

ABOUT SIDING

The "siding" is the outside surfacing material that is nailed over the sheathing. Popular types are shingles, clapboards and board and batten (vertical) siding. (If board and batten is used, extending all the way down to the sill on the foundation, it provides a lock-together effect similar to that of downward-extended sheathing. So the sheathing need not extend below the sole plate.)

In most cases, the same type of siding is used on the addition as was used on the house, though in many instances a different type may be used to advantage. This is often the case when the addition is obviously an addition—frequently true of country homes that have been enlarged over the years. Frequently, for example, a rambling clapboard house will have an addition with board and batten siding—a combination that's sometimes more attractive than matching, especially if the addition is considerably smaller than the original house. Another advantage of board and batten lies in the fact that it's often available in 4'-wide panel form, eliminating much of the work of applying it. Unless siding matched to the existing house is essential, ask your lumber dealer about panel-type siding.

Shingled Walls

If you're applying shingles to the outside walls of your addition, you'll probably use them over "backer board." This is an insulating, water-resistant fiber-type board sold in strips suited to shingle length. You nail it to the sheathing at the bottom, with a wood strip under the bottom edge to tilt the first course of shingles out. From there on up, after nailing the shingles in place, you nail on another strip of backer board—so the next course of shingles will overlap it at the bottom by about $1/2''$. The backer board makes the whole job more weatherproof, adds to the wall's insulation and makes more visible shadow lines between courses of shingles.

THE CEILING

Assuming the ceiling is to be a conventional horizontal (not sloped) one, the ceiling joists are mounted on top of the double plate and should run parallel to the floor joists. This calls for an inside wall or other support directly above the girder that runs under the floor. (If you examine the average house, you'll find that its upper floors are divided by walls running directly (or almost directly) above the basement girder. This provides a continuous line of vertical support from the ground up. This is a basic essential. If the structure (house or addition) is narrow enough not to require a girder for central support of the joists, continuous joists may be used rather than overlapped ones, and central walls are not needed.

16

FRAMING THE ROOF

THINGS YOU SHOULD KNOW

Assembling the Roof

One of the easiest ways to start a gabled roof-framing job is to nail a few ceiling joists in place first and brace them temporarily to serve as support for a temporary plywood working platform. (This technique is shown in the photos in chapter 24.) The plywood can be nailed to the joists in a few places with duplex head nails that can be pulled out later. Only a few panels of plywood are necessary, and they can be moved from one working area to another, as the work progresses, by merely pulling and redriving the temporary nails.

As the do-it-yourselfer seldom has a crew working with him, the roof-framing job is usually easiest if the "ridge board" is erected first, lightly nailed to temporary supports. (The ridge board is the board that runs along the peak of the roof, with rafters joining it on both sides.) Once the ridge board is on its temporary supports, it's a simple matter to nail the rafters in place at pre-marked spacings. The temporary ridge-board supports should be so lo-

cated, however, as not to be in the way of rafters to come. Start the rafter work with the end rafters, as they should be fairly close to the end support, so the ridge board will be reasonably firm at their points of attachment. Follow with rafters near the intermediate temporary supports for the same reason. Nail both joists and rafters as shown in the nailing drawings. It is essential, of course, to install joists at each rafter location (if not already there) as the work progresses. When the starting rafters and joists are in place near the temporary supports, the ridge board should be firm enough to make the installation of the intervening rafters easy work. If the roof peak is a high one, you may need a stepladder to reach the ridge for nailing. If so, be sure the temporary platform on which it rests is firmly anchored. If you plan to floor the attic completely, anyway, do it before the rafter job begins, and allow space for the rafters.

Rafter Spans and Sizes

The span of a roof rafter is the *horizon-*

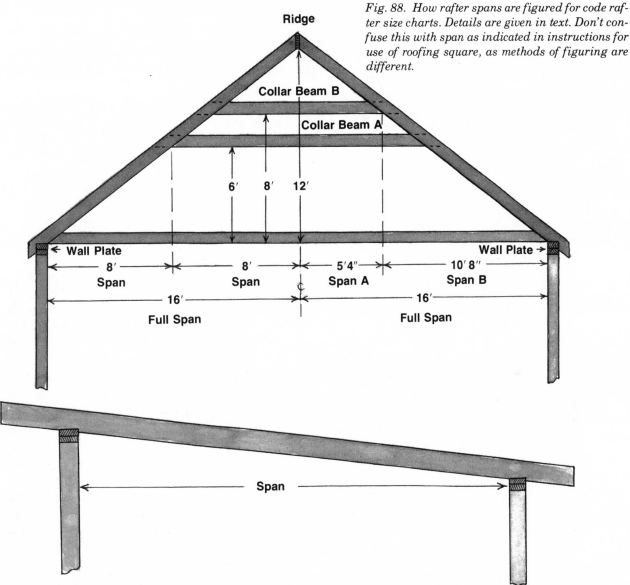

Fig. 88. *How rafter spans are figured for code rafter size charts. Details are given in text. Don't confuse this with span as indicated in instructions for use of roofing square, as methods of figuring are different.*

Collar Beam B

Collar Beam A

6' 8' 12'

Wall Plate   Wall Plate

| 8' | 8' | 5'4" | 10'8" |
| Span | Span | Span A | Span B |

16'   16'

Full Span   Full Span

Span

Fig. 89. *On shed roof, span is measured between inner surfaces of supports, such as the plates atop supporting walls.*

tal distance between its points of support, even though the rafter may have a steep pitch. The *length* of the rafter must not be confused with the span. As shown in the diagram, the use of collar beams reduces the span. If, for example, the span of a rafter in a gabled roof is 16', and a collar

beam is used between the rafters at the midpoint of the span, the span is reduced to 8', making possible the use of rafters with considerably smaller cross section and corresponding reduction in cost.

Except where unusually heavy snow loads are encountered, rafter spans may be

Framing the Roof   95

somewhat greater than floor joist spans of the same size lumber. As local codes are commonly matched to local conditions, your best guide is the local code if there is one. Otherwise you can safely use the table of floor joist spans and sizes. If snow loads are not great, you might cut costs by using the following rafter size table:

Rafter size in inches	Center-to-center spacing (in inches)	Maximum span (in feet)
2 x 4	12	8
	16	7
	24	5' 9"
2 x 6	12	12' 6"
	16	10' 9"
	24	9
2 x 8	12	16
	16	14
	24	12
2 x 10	12	20
	16	18
	24	15
2 x 12	12	24
	16	21
	24	18

THE GABLED ROOF

Typically, the ceiling joists and the roof rafters are cut and nailed in place as shown in the detail drawings. The pros lay out the rafter end cuts with a "rafter square." This is a large steel square stamped with tables and graduated markings that enable you to lay out not only rafter cuts, but also stairway stringers (the notched side members of a stairway). A little practice is advisable, however, before using the square on the actual job, as some concentration is necessary in learning to use it properly. If you'd like to master this tool, you can buy a brand like the Stanley Rafter Square, for which a 46-page instruction booklet is available. Once you have the knack, the rafter square is easy to use.

One of the easiest ways to mark for ceiling joist and rafter cuts, however, is by laying them out full size on flat ground and marking them for the actual cuts, as shown in the drawing. A little shifting of the various members may be necessary to line them up, but complications are unlikely. You need to know the height the roof ridge is to be above the attic floor and the distance between the plates on which the ceiling joists and rafters will rest. After you've cut the first pair of rafters and joists, fit them together on the ground for a tryout and check all dimensions. If all's well, use these members as patterns for marking and cutting all the others. If any correction is necessary, make it before further marking and cutting.

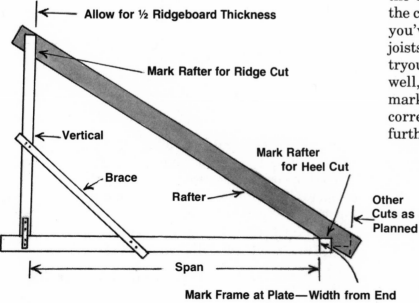

Allow for ½ Ridgeboard Thickness

Mark Rafter for Ridge Cut

Vertical

Mark Rafter for Heel Cut

Brace

Rafter

Other Cuts as Planned

Span

Mark Frame at Plate—Width from End

Fig. 90. One easy way to cut rafters is with a full size mock-up made from lumber that will later be used in addition framing. Brace vertical member as shown. Height of vertical member should equal height of planned roof. Simply lay the mock-up (shown white) on top of the lumber for rafter (shown gray) and mark for cuts at ridge and at plate (heel cut) and cut to shape accordingly. Try first rafter for correct fit. If OK, use it as pattern for other rafters.

Fig. 91. Heel cuts in rafters. Note that circular saw cuts a little beyond corner because of blade form. To avoid overcut, you can use sabre saw.

Fig. 93. How rafters fit against ridge board, as viewed from inside. Collar beam is shown between rafters. Most codes don't require collar beams at each rafter, but at every second or third rafter. Check local regulations.

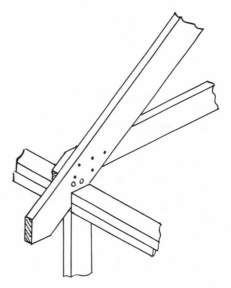

Fig. 92. Nailing rafter and ceiling joist at plate. Use five 3" nails through rafter into joist (or vice versa). Joist and rafter are toenailed to plate with 3" nails, two through joist and two through rafter on other side.

Fig. 94. When roof rafters are in place, studs are installed in gable ends from wall plate to end rafters. These studs are notched at top so their outer surface is flush with end rafters. Sheathing is then nailed to rafters and studs. Note use of temporary diagonal bracing on wall. If wall is sheathed before this stage, bracing isn't required.

Framing the Roof   97

THE SHED ROOF

The shed roof, sometimes called a lean-to roof, slopes in only one direction, from the high side to the low side. On an addition to a house, the high side is usually attached to the house wall or roof, so the roof slopes downward away from the house. This type of roof is much simpler, more economical and easier to build than a gabled roof, but it's not suitable for all additions. Because of its advantages, however, it's worth considering when planning your addition.

If the rafters start from an existing roof, their spacing should correspond to that of the rafters in the existing roof, so the new rafters can be nailed through the existing roof into the old rafters. Short vertical struts of 2 x 4 may be used between the point of attachment of the new rafters down to the plate or ceiling joists below, to add rigidity, especially if the point of attachment is a considerable distance from the eaves of the existing roof.

The easiest way to mark the rafter ends for cutting is by propping a length of rafter stock with its upper end against the end of

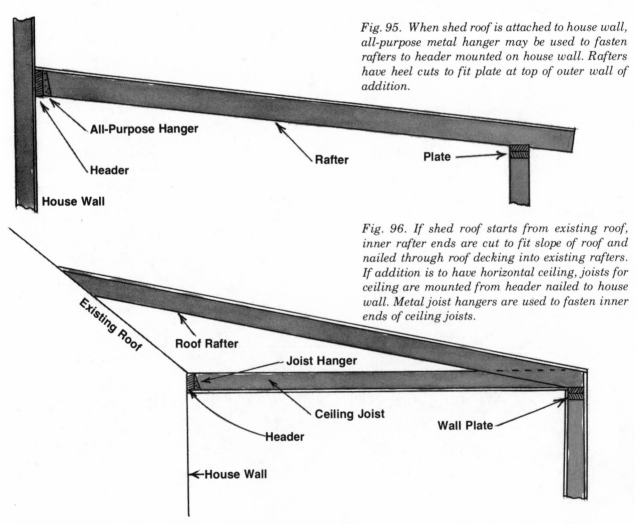

Fig. 95. When shed roof is attached to house wall, all-purpose metal hanger may be used to fasten rafters to header mounted on house wall. Rafters have heel cuts to fit plate at top of outer wall of addition.

All-Purpose Hanger

Header

House Wall

Rafter

Plate

Fig. 96. If shed roof starts from existing roof, inner rafter ends are cut to fit slope of roof and nailed through roof decking into existing rafters. If addition is to have horizontal ceiling, joists for ceiling are mounted from header nailed to house wall. Metal joist hangers are used to fasten inner ends of ceiling joists.

Existing Roof

Roof Rafter

Joist Hanger

Ceiling Joist

Header

Wall Plate

House Wall

the existing roof and its lower end against the wall plate of the new addition. (It may be necessary to nail it temporarily.) It may then be pencil-marked along the actual roof line and plate for accurate cutting. After cutting along the marked lines, try the rafter in the location it will occupy. If you've marked carefully, it should fit perfectly. If it doesn't, trim or shim it so it does. Then use it as a pattern for all the other rafters.

If the shed roof rafters start from the wall of the house, a "header" must first be mounted on the wall at the rafter starting point. This is of nominal 2″ lumber, usually in the same width as the rafters. There are two ways of mounting the header. In one, the siding is removed from the wall in a strip as wide as the header, exposing the sheathing along the path the header will occupy. The header may then be nailed through the sheathing into the studding inside the wall. In another somewhat easier method, the siding is not removed. Instead, the header is nailed through both siding and sheathing into the wall studs. In the case of slant-surfaced siding like shingles or clapboard, a layer of siding is sometimes added with the bevel reversed (as a piece of bevel siding upside down) so as to provide a vertical surface rather than a slanted one to which to nail the header. The studs inside the wall can be located from the outside by drilling a few holes through the siding and sheathing below the header level. Except in very old houses, location of one or two studs serves to establish the spacing of the others. In very old

Fig. 97. Metal framing fasteners. Left, all-purpose fastener can be used to fasten rafters to header on house wall, as it adjusts to pitch angles. Center, post mounting fastener locks vertical wood post to masonry base, can be adjusted to adapt to off-center mounting bolt. Right, joist hanger is used to fasten joists to header, etc. Instructions accompany some brands. If they're lacking, get needed information where you buy.

Fig. 98. Shed-roofed dormer is framed like this, in either old or new roof. Rafters on each side of dormer opening are doubled. Doubled header supports intermediate rafter ends above dormer. Doubled sill does same job below dormer. If dormer is being added to existing roof, plan work so opening can be closed in case of rain before dormer is completed.

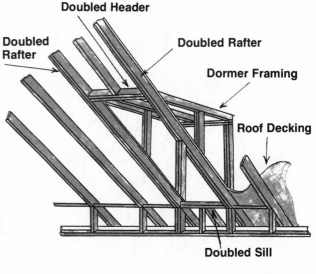

Doubled Header

Doubled Rafter

Doubled Rafter

Dormer Framing

Roof Decking

Doubled Sill

houses, however, the stud spacing sometimes varies even in the same wall. So stud locations should be checked by drilling. If you have any doubts, regardless of the age of the house, check by drilling. The drilled holes can be as small as ⅛″. If the drill passes through the siding and sheathing and then slips all the way in quickly, you haven't hit a stud. If it encounters continued resistance after reaching the depth of siding and sheathing thickness, you are drilling into a stud or other framing member.

Ceiling joists may be used to provide a horizontal ceiling, just as with a gabled roof. If so, they're mounted from a header on the house to the wall plate just as the rafters are.

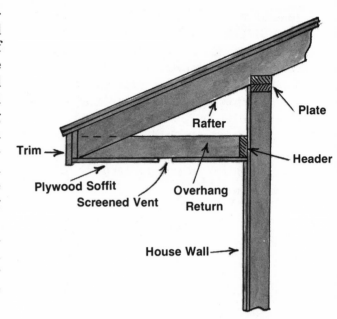

Fig. 100. Where roof has overhang, construction is like this. Screened vents release water vapor without admitting insects.

Fig. 99. Rafter ends support roof overhang, like this. Here, stud and rafter spacing are the same. Rafters are often spaced farther apart than studs.

ROOF DECKING

Unless otherwise specified by local code, you can use ½″ plywood to cover your roof framing, mounting it so that seams between panels occur along the midline of a rafter. Nailing is usually with 2½″ (8d, eight-penny) nails spaced about 5″ or 6″ apart along panel edges and about 10″ apart into intermediate rafters. Any of the common rafter spacings result in rafter centers matched to plywood panel widths and lengths with one or more rafters between the panel edges. Simply measure for the intermediate rafters and draw pencil lines with a straight edge to show the nailing lines. Before starting the nailing, be sure panel edges are centered on rafters to allow for the adjoining panels.

THE TYPES OF ROOFING

If your addition has a low-pitched roof (economical to build and easy to work on), your best bet for surfacing it is roll roofing. This is available with or without mineral coating (like fine sand). If you apply it according to the manufacturer's instructions with cold roof cement in all seams, you can have a good roof with a pitch as little as 1" per foot. Major manufacturers of roofing such as Bird & Son offer this type of roofing in a variety of colors, including black, white, green and red. The lighter the color, the cooler the space under the roof, something to keep in mind if you plan to air-condition. The availability of different colors, of course, is important if you must match your roofing to existing roofing. The surface of a low-pitched roof, however, is usually not readily visible from ground level, so a reasonable color approximation is often adequate.

For shingles, you must have a steeper pitch. Some types can be used with a pitch as little as 2" per foot if a double layer of 15 lb. asphalt felt (like tarpaper) is applied first. Generally, however, a pitch of at least 4" per foot is to be favored, with a single layer of the asphalt felt under the shingles. Whatever type of roofing you use, follow the instructions that come with it, as the methods of application vary considerably from one brand to another, and failure to follow them can cause unsatisfactory results.

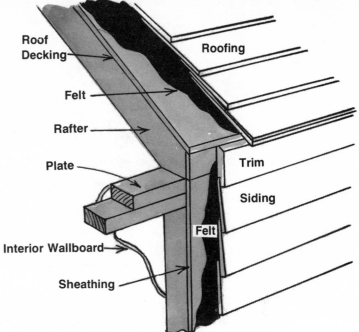

Fig. 101. Where roof is built with only enough overhang for rain gutter, construction is like this. Use of roofing felt (asphalt impregnated) under roofing and siding aids in damp-proofing, is especially important under shingles of relatively low-pitched roofs. Attic vapor venting is usually through screened and louvered vents in gable ends.

Fig. 102. If your addition will have cathedral ceiling, insulation must be stapled between rafters like this, unless insulating board or foam is used on top of roof decking, under roofing. Plastic sheeting (visible on end wall) is stapled over framing after insulation is installed, to act as vapor seal. This is important to prevent interior moisture (as from kitchen, bath, etc.) from penetrating wall and damaging exterior paint.

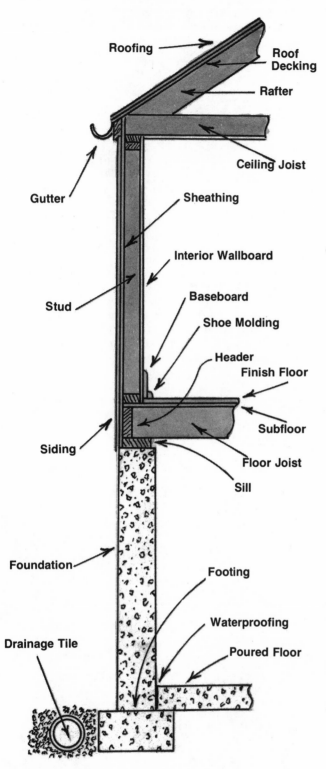

Roofing

Roof Decking

Rafter

Ceiling Joist

Gutter

Sheathing

Interior Wallboard

Stud

Baseboard

Shoe Molding

Header

Finish Floor

Siding

Subfloor

Floor Joist

Sill

Foundation

Footing

Waterproofing

Drainage Tile

Poured Floor

Fig. 103. Typical construction from footing to roof applies to additions and outbuildings of major size. Poured floor isn't needed in crawl space, but plastic sheeting should be used over earth surface to seal out dampness.

When You Buy Shingles

When you buy shingles for your roof or walls, you'll usually be buying a "square." This is the amount of material needed to cover 100 square feet, when used *as specified*. Possible variations result from the "exposure" of the shingles, as each "course" of shingles overlaps the course below it by a certain distance. The exposure is the length of shingle actually exposed to the weather—not protected by the overlap of the next course above it. In general, wooden shingles are applied with much less exposure when they're used on the roof than when they're used on the walls, as the roof takes much more of a beating from the elements. Too much exposure on a roof could shorten shingle life by permitting cupping and splitting. The important point: Follow the instructions that come with the shingles you buy. If there are no instructions, ask for the information you need when you buy. There's quite a bit of variation in shingles, so be sure to get the data for the brand you'll use. For the most part, asphalt composition shingles have precise instructions printed on the package. In any event, one or more layers of 15 lb. asphalt felt, stapled to the roof and overlapped in shingle fashion as described earlier, as an under-layer, will make your roof less subject to leaks.

ABOUT FLASHING

Metal "flashing" is used to waterproof roof junctures, as where different slopes of a roof meet, or where the roof joins a wall. The commonest metal flashing is soft aluminum, which is relatively inexpensive, easy to shape and cut, and easy to nail, as the nails can be driven through it without first drilling holes. It is always applied in such a manner as to deflect rainwater away from seams and onto the surface of the roofing. Typically, it might be slipped up under a wall clapboard (or course of shingles) and bent outward on top of the roofing. The drawings show the usual methods of using flashing to meet typical roof situations.

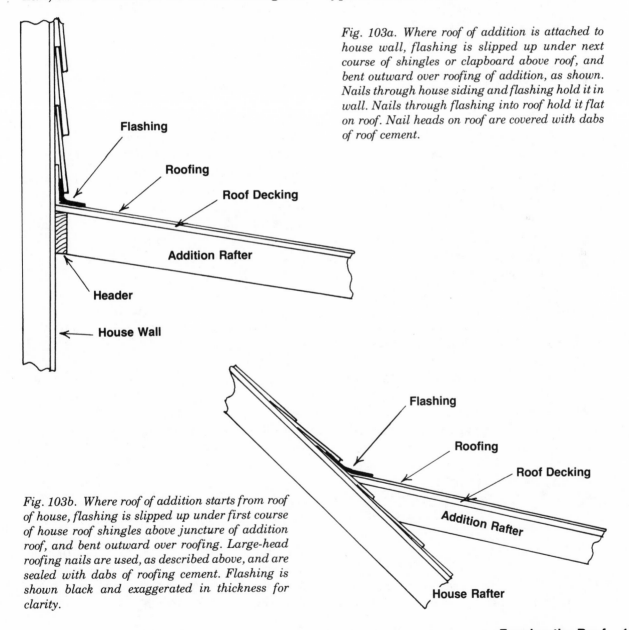

Fig. 103a. Where roof of addition is attached to house wall, flashing is slipped up under next course of shingles or clapboard above roof, and bent outward over roofing of addition, as shown. Nails through house siding and flashing hold it in wall. Nails through flashing into roof hold it flat on roof. Nail heads on roof are covered with dabs of roof cement.

Flashing

Roofing

Roof Decking

Addition Rafter

Header

House Wall

Flashing

Roofing

Roof Decking

Addition Rafter

House Rafter

Fig. 103b. Where roof of addition starts from roof of house, flashing is slipped up under first course of house roof shingles above juncture of addition roof, and bent outward over roofing. Large-head roofing nails are used, as described above, and are sealed with dabs of roofing cement. Flashing is shown black and exaggerated in thickness for clarity.

17

DOING THE INTERIOR WORK

Once your addition is enclosed and roofed, you can start on the inside. Typically, the plumbing and electrical work is installed (see chapters 18 and 19), then the insulation; then after cleaning up, the wallboard is put up.

You apply wallboard in much the same manner as the sheathing, but you use nails made for the purpose (buy them where you buy the wallboard) and follow the instructions of the brand of wallboard you're using. For most living areas you'll probably be using gypsum board, which has the general qualities of a plastered wall when completed but has relatively little insulating effect. Where maximum insulation is essential, as in some attics, you may prefer an insulating fiber-type wallboard. This is softer and more easily dented, but it's much lighter in weight and has considerably greater insulating effect.

GYPSUM BOARD

This type of wallboard may be code-required in certain types of installation, as in an attached garage, because of its fire resistance. Check your local code before you select your wallboard.

As the seams between wallboard panels must be located at framing members, such as studs, look the wall framing over and plan your wallboard panel arrangement in advance. Usually, you start from a corner and cut the first panel so the outer edge comes at the center of a stud. If you're using a type with tapered edges (made for use with a seam tape system), cut the panel so that the cut edge is in the corner, the tapered edge at the stud, as that's where you'll have to make a smooth seam at a later stage. If your wallboard is the common $1/2''$ thickness, use $1\,5/8''$ nails, spaced $8''$ apart on walls, $7''$ apart on ceilings. Drive these nails into every stud or ceiling joist and be sure the wallboard is pressed tightly against the framing while the nailing is being done. To hold the wallboard against ceiling joists, unless you have a crew of helpers, you make a T-shaped prop of 2 x 4 lumber, braced diagonally to keep the cross bar of the T from wobbling. As the T has to be a little less than full ceiling height, you'll still need a helper to push it up as you nail, but the job usually progresses without problems. On walls, of course, the wallboard is simply stood up against the framing (after being cut to size) and nailed.

Cutting Gypsum Board

A pair of sawhorses is very useful in cutting gypsum board to width or length. Lay the panel of gypsum board on top of the sawhorses and pencil-mark the cutting line on the surface that will be the visible wall surface. Then, using a straight piece of lumber as a guide, score the line with a sharp, pointed knife like a Stanley trimming knife. The offcut piece can then be "clicked" free simply by pressing down on it, with the edge of a sawhorse directly under the scored line. (The procedure is similar to that used in glass cutting.) Once the offcut piece snaps free along the line, you can use the same trimming knife to sever the paper backing on the rear surface of the wallboard, freeing the offcut piece entirely.

The Seams

Most gypsum board seams today are of the taped variety. The wallboard edges are tapered or recessed. After the wallboard has been nailed in place, the tapered or recessed edges are filled with joint cement (made for the purpose) of a buttery consistency. The seam tape is then smoothed into the surface of the fresh cement, usually with a broad putty knife, but follow the instructions of the manufacturer. A thin layer of cement is then applied over the tape to complete the first stage of the job, in most systems. When this first stage has hardened, usually overnight, it is fine-sanded, and a second coat of cement is applied over it, feathered out in a very thin layer at least 2″ away from each side of the tape. When this hardens, you sand it smooth and apply a third very thin coat, feathering out further, sanding when hard. Typically, this third coat, sanded (always with fine sandpaper), completes the job. If it's all done carefully, the seam is invisible after painting or papering.

When the instructions that accompany the wallboard you use vary from the above, follow the wallboard instructions. The seam systems may differ somewhat with the brand. If you'd prefer to avoid the seam work, you can turn it over to a professional. Just look in the Yellow Pages of your local phone book under "Dry Wall Contractors." You can hire one to do the seam work after you've hung the wallboard, or have him do the wallboard job. If you want only the seam work done, however, you must do the wallboard job right.

ABOUT TRIM

You may want to match your addition's flooring and interior trim (as around windows and doorways) to that of the existing house. If so, look at the flooring and trim available from your lumberyard—and if you don't see what you want, ask if it can be had on order. It's usually possible to make your needs known by description. Often the lumberyard can show you diagrams of special molding types not ordinarily stocked. If your house is an older one, it may have trim styles not widely used today.

ABOUT FLOORING

If you want wood flooring, such as oak, look into both conventional and pre-finished types. The prefinished types should not be laid until all other interior work is completed, to avoid marring. Regular flooring can be sanded (with a rented floor sander) and finished with any of the usual floor finishes, ranging from shellac to polyurethane. (Ask your local paint store for the pros and cons.) Shellac is quick drying, economical and easy to apply, but it tends to darken with time, and it isn't waterproof. Polyurethane finishes are extremely durable and highly water resistant but usually somewhat slower drying. And that doesn't end the list.

Nailing Machines

If you plan to lay your own flooring, ask your supplier about a nailing machine. Many lumberyards (if you buy your flooring from them) will lend you a nailing machine to simplify laying the flooring. You pay a deposit, use the machine to do the job and get your deposit back when you return the machine. Other yards simply rent the machines.

The need for this tool stems from the fact that most finished flooring is "blind nailed" so no nail heads show in the finished floor except in the first strip laid and the last one or two strips laid. To achieve this result, the nails are driven at an angle through the edge of each flooring strip, into the subfloor.

The flooring strips are of tongue-and-groove form, with a groove along one edge and a projecting tongue along the other. The strips are laid so the tongue of one edge fits into the groove of the adjacent one. Most flooring is also "end matched," which means that the ends of the flooring strips are also tongued and grooved, so the tongue across the end of one strip will fit into the groove across the end of the next strip, to which it joins. This makes for a smooth, even floor surface with no edges or ends above-level.

If there's any chance of dampness from below, cover the subfloor with 15 lb. asphalt felt overlapped 4″ at the seams, before the finished flooring work begins.

To start, you nail the first flooring strip through its upper surface, with its grooved edge a fraction of an inch from the wall to allow for possible expansion of the flooring. The nails through the surface of the first strip should be close enough to the wall-edge to be covered and concealed by the shoe molding around the base of the wall. The other (outer) edge is then toenailed through the tongue into the floor. This is where you use the nailing machine. It holds the nails in driving position at exactly the right angle (45 or 50 degrees) with their tips in exact position for driving through the corner of the tongue into the subfloor. Most of these nailing machines or "nailers" carry a supply of flooring nails (typically 150) and are simply struck with a hammer on top of the nail-driving plunger. As the operation varies somewhat with the brand, get instructions where you get the tool. If your flooring supplier doesn't have a lend or rental arrangement, the chances are you can rent a floor nailer from a tool rental agency. Inquire, in any event, if the nailer requires its own type of nails. Some do. Others use standard flooring nails.

When you reach the last strip of flooring, you must again nail it straight down through the upper surface, as there isn't room between the strip and the wall to use the nailing machine. Depending on the machine, it may be necessary to nail the last two strips in this manner.

VI

Installing Your Plumbing and Wiring

Fig. 104. Rigid and flexible plastic pipe and fittings. The rigid form is used for interior water supply and drainage plumbing and is connected with fittings bonded in place with solvent cement. Flexible plastic pipe is widely used for outside underground water supply lines, also in wells. Connections are made with special fittings forced into flexible pipe ends and held with stainless steel clamps. Be sure to specify the type of use intended when you buy. For hot water, use only type made for the purpose and set water heater thermostat to keep safe range. NATIONAL SANITATION FOUNDATION

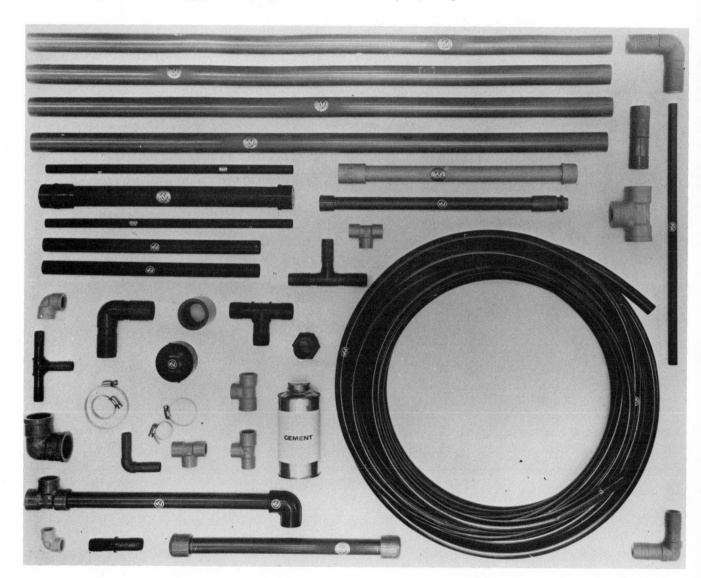

18

HOW TO DO YOUR OWN PLUMBING

If your addition involves plumbing, as for a kitchen or bathroom, you'll be happy to know that plumbing work is far easier today than it was in the past—thanks to new materials like plastic pipe. And it's not difficult to plan the job when you know the basic principles. It's extremely important, however, to familiarize yourself with your local code (if any), as plumbing codes vary like other codes and may differ in certain important ways, especially regarding the drainage and waste system, as described shortly. The water supply system, for most do-it-yourselfers, is the easiest part of the job, as the pipes are small and can be run through the house structure almost as simply as wiring.

THE DRAINAGE SYSTEM

The drainage system must be planned in advance, as its pipes are larger and must slope $1/4''$ per foot along their lateral runs to the vertical "soil stack" or smaller "drain stack." And the drainage system must be "vented." This means that vent pipes (connected to the drainage pipe system) must run upward through the roof and have their upper ends (above the roof) open to the atmosphere. You have probably seen these pipes extending through the roofs of many houses, including your own, often directly above the kitchen and bathrooms. They serve several very important purposes. For one, they admit air to the drainage system to replace out-flowing water. You can demonstrate the need for this with a simple soda-straw experiment. Just stand the soda straw in a tall glass of water, press your fingertip tightly over the soda straw's upper end and lift it out. The water in the straw will remain in it. But when you release your fingertip from the top of the straw, the water flows out freely because air can enter to replace it. Lack of venting, of course, would not stop the water from flowing out of your drainage pipes, but it would slow the out-flow considerably. And it could create a more serious problem. The suction effect created in the piping by the outflowing water would pull replacement air into the system through the "traps" under your fixtures like sinks and wash basins. (Traps are the

S-curved sections of pipes under fixtures. They are designed to provide a water seal against sewer gas.) You can actually hear the glugging sound as air is drawn through the traps in an improperly vented drainage system. (It can also happen, though rarely, in properly vented systems under certain conditions.) The danger in this situation results when enough water is sucked out of the trap to break its water seal. One other important reason for venting lies in the possibility of gas pressure build-up in the sewer system. Without venting, the gas could force its way through the traps into the house. The rest of the drainage system is merely based on the simple fact that water flows downhill.

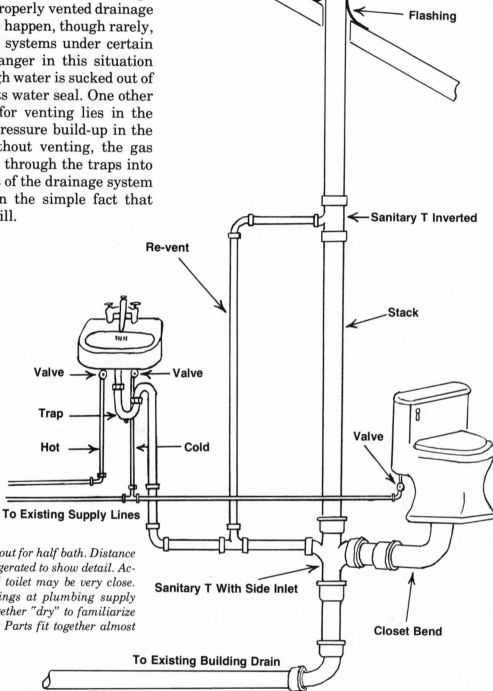

Fig. 105. Plumbing layout for half bath. Distance between fixtures is exaggerated to show detail. Actually, wash basin and toilet may be very close. Examine pipe and fittings at plumbing supply house, and fit them together "dry" to familiarize yourself with assembly. Parts fit together almost like a kit.

In general, the closer fixtures like sinks, basins and toilets are to the vertical soil stack, the better. Here, your local code is likely to specify just how far from the stack a fixture may be, or how far away it may be without a "re-vent." A re-vent is a small vent pipe extending upward from a fixture drain to a connection to the soil stack at a point above the fixture. Sometimes the re-vent itself is extended up through the roof, becoming a separate vent pipe. Typically, a re-vent is required if the drain line (to the soil stack) is more than 42″ long, though the distance may vary with some codes. The details are shown in the diagrams.

PLANNING YOUR PLUMBING

In planning, much depends on the existing layout of your house drainage plumbing. (You can run water supply pipes almost anywhere.) Smaller drainage pipes, as from a kitchen sink, are less likely to present problems than large pipes, as from a toilet. In many cases, the simplest answer is an extra soil stack connected into the main house drain (which leads to the house sewer). The trick here is in picking the easiest way to connect the new stack to the existing system. In many cases, this can be done at an existing "clean out" fitting, as shown in the diagram. Another clean out is then added beyond the connection. Unless the new stack is inside of the existing house wall (where it attaches), it will probably be necessary to make an opening in the existing foundation for the soil pipe to pass through. This should be planned well in advance and done at the most suitable stage of the addition work. You can rent an "impact drill" from a tool rental agency to make the opening. The usual method consists of drilling a number of closely spaced holes in a circle, then breaking out the concrete between them with a cold chisel to make the full-sized opening. You can also rent a power chisel to use instead of the hammer-driven cold chisel. Rental charges for the impact drill and power chisel are usually reasonable.

Fig. 106. Where to connect new plumbing (like half bath) to existing system. Normally, your existing plumbing will have a clean out plug near point where building drain leaves house. It may be at end of lateral run, like this.

Fig. 107. To connect new plumbing to plumbing in Fig. 106, replace clean out with sanitary T (or other appropriate fitting) like this, and add new clean out plug. If you are connecting a different type of pipe (as plastic to cast iron), adapter fitting is used at (A).

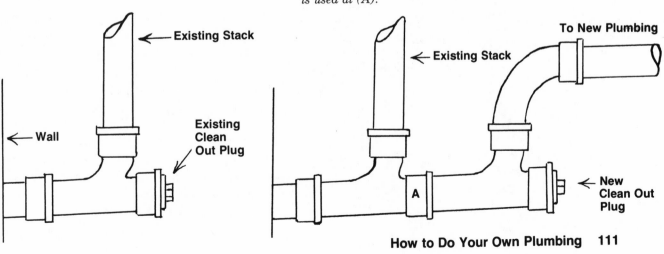

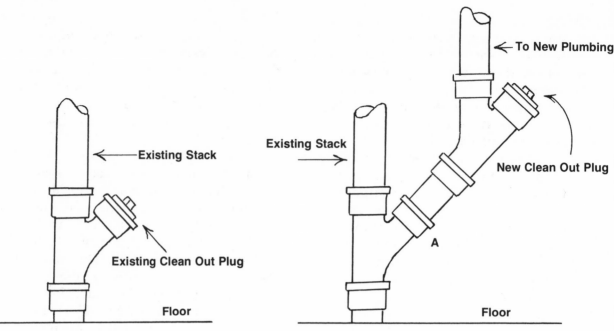

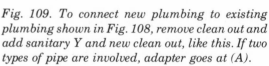

Fig. 108. Existing clean out plug may be in vertical run of pipe, like this, if house drain runs through basement floor rather than wall.

Fig. 109. To connect new plumbing to existing plumbing shown in Fig. 108, remove clean out and add sanitary Y and new clean out, like this. If two types of pipe are involved, adapter goes at (A).

Fig. 110. How drainage and waste system is mounted in house structure. For clarity, framing is shown without walls or subfloor. This assembly would serve two baths on opposite sides of wall that contains the soil stack—a pipe- and labor-saving arrangement. Wall containing stack is framed with 2 x 6 lumber to allow width for stack through sole. Lavatory sink drain connections are at left, toilet drain connections at center, tub or shower drain connections at right. NATIONAL SANITATION FOUNDATION

If the new soil stack is very close to the existing house wall (or against it), you may be able to lead the connecting soil pipe through the header or end joist of the existing house floor. This depends on the individual situation, dimensions of the joists, type of pipe, etc. Often, if you have the actual pipe fittings that would be used (such as an elbow, closet bend, sanitary T or Y branch), you can try it in place to see if the job is feasible—before you cut into the framing. If you have to cut holes in tight quarters for a large pipe (drainage) to pass through joists, a sabre saw with a swiveling blade (like the Sears Scroller) makes it possible when it couldn't be done with an ordinary sabre saw. If the job calls for a smaller hole, as for water supply pipe, you can buy a right angle attachment for your standard power drill. This lets you bore any size hole the drill can handle at right angles to the drill, allowing you to work in spaces far shorter than would be possible without the attachment. Check into these tools and their prices before you tackle your plumbing work. Both can be used for many other jobs later on. The right angle attachment for the power drill also comes in handy very often in wiring work. An important point to keep in mind if you run pipes through joists is that nails will be driven upward into the lower edges of the joists if wallboard is applied, as in the case of a finished ceiling. Be sure your pipe holes (through the joists) are far enough above the bottom edges of the joists to be safe from nail punctures. Nails can puncture copper and plastic pipe. Where pipes must be close to the bottom edges of the joists, or where they are set in notches in the wall studs, they can be protected from nail puncture by nailing iron plates to the framing members at the pipe locations, as shown in the photo. Nails that might otherwise puncture the pipes are stopped by the iron plates and can then be pulled out and relocated. Nail puncture problems stem from the fact that pipe locations are often "lost" when the wallboard is applied.

Suspended Plumbing

In basements that are not to have a finished ceiling (or where a "dropped" ceil-

Fig. 111. Looking up at under-floor drain and waste pipes. Elbow through floor at left leads to toilet flange. Pipe in foreground leads to stack. Small elbow through floor at right is for lavatory sink drain.

Fig. 112. Plastic drain pipe leading from tub trap. Copper water supply lines (lower right) are used in this installation. Note electrical cable also led through joists.

Fig. 113. In-wall plastic plumbing. Soil stack is at center. Hole through floor for toilet connection below floor is at lower left. Drain line for lavatory sink enters stack from right. Drain for kitchen sink enters stack slightly lower, from left. Note galvanized metal plates mounted on studding and sole to prevent wallboard nails from puncturing pipes.

ing will be installed below the joists), lateral runs of pipe are often installed below the joists, supported by pipe hangers, pipe strap or wood frames. The same applies to crawl spaces. This, of course, simplifies the installation of the pipe. The length of the supports is adjusted to provide the pitch (slope) required. The pitch is essential for the proper functioning of drain pipes at all times. Water supply pipes should also be pitched downward toward a system drain valve to facilitate draining the water supply system if the house is to be left unheated in winter. About the same pitch as is used in drain lines is adequate. It is not necessary to have the new water supply system in your addition pitch down to the same drain valves as the existing water pipes as long as both old and new water piping can be completely drained through one or more drain valves.

As drainage pipe fittings are designed to allow for a pitch of ¼" per foot where they connect to vertical pipes, plan your plumbing accordingly. The branch of a drainage T, for example, is slightly tipped away from right angles to allow for connecting a vertical pipe to a lateral one that's pitched downward to it. A water supply pipe T, on the other hand, is branched at 90 degrees. As water supply pipes are smaller, however, an almost imperceptible flex is all that's needed to provide the necessary pitch for easy draining.

THE TYPES OF PIPE

Local code permitting, you have a choice of plastic, copper, steel or cast iron pipe for your drainage plumbing. Except for cast iron, the same choice applies to your water supply piping. Unless your local code requires it, you do not have to use the same type of pipe in your addition as was used in the existing house. There are fittings that enable you to interconnect the different types.

PLASTIC PIPE

Plastic pipe is understandably popular because of its light weight and easy working qualities. You can, for example, *carry* all the drainage pipe, including vent pipes and fittings, for an average house under

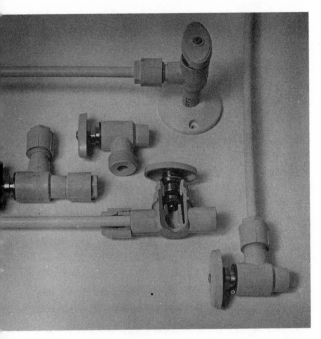

Fig. 114. Valves are also made in plastic, for use with plastic pipe or with adapting connections for use with other types. GENOVA

Fig. 115. Sample plastic drainage pipe sizes and soil pipe fittings. Some fitting types available in plastic are not available in metal. GENOVA

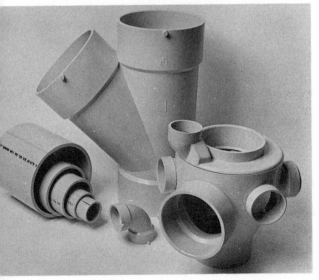

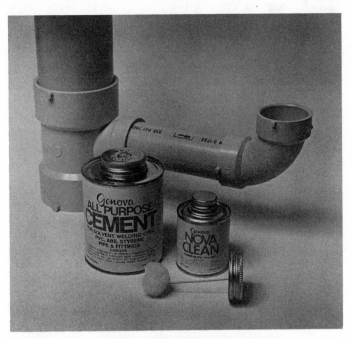

Fig. 116. Typical drain connection to sanitary T in stack, as might be used to connect sink drain to stack. In foreground, cleaner to prepare pipe and fittings for connection and cement for solvent-welding the connection. Cement is applied with applicator attached to can cap, as shown. GENOVA

your arms. In one more trip, you can carry all the plastic water supply pipe.

You can cut the pipe with almost any saw, but a hacksaw is usually preferred because its finer teeth make a smooth cut. It takes less than 10 seconds to cut a 1/2" plastic water pipe, about half a minute to cut 1 1/2" drain pipe. Larger-diameter plastic soil pipe can be cut in proportionate time. If there are any rough edges or burrs on the cut ends that might cause snagging of drainage material in the pipe, just smooth them off with sandpaper before the assembly work begins.

You join the pipe to fittings (such as elbows, T's, etc.) with "solvent cement." This is a chemical preparation that not only cements the connection but also partially dissolves the close-fitting surfaces so

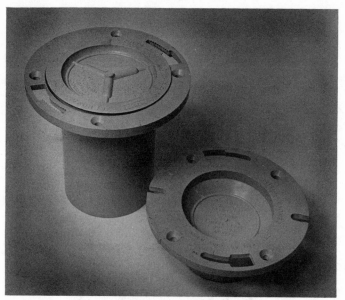

Fig. 117. Plastic toilet flanges. As with metal flanges, screws go into floor through countersunk holes. Toilet mounting bolts are inserted head down in wide portion of slots in rim. Threaded portion of bolts extends up through base of toilet bowl to take nuts that hold toilet to floor. Wax gasket between bowl and flange seals the connection. Plumbing suppliers stock the gaskets. Toilet bowl is given slight turn to slide bolt heads into narrow portion of slot, where they hold while nuts are tightened. Very important: mount toilet flange so that toilet will be in correct position after slight turn required. Plastic toilet flanges have an exclusive feature—knockout disk that seals out sewer gases until toilet is mounted. You break out the disk just before toilet is mounted on flange. GENOVA

Fig. 118. You can cut any residential-size plastic pipe with a fine-toothed wood saw or hacksaw. To assure a right-angle cut, you can use a miter box, as shown.

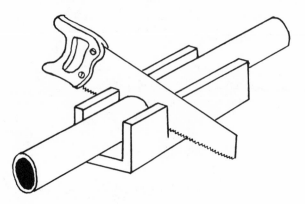

that they actually fuse together. But you have to work fast and with care, as the solvent-cemented connection begins to firm up in about half a minute and can't be shifted after that. The best method is that of assembling the connection "dry" and marking it for position before making the final solvent-cemented connection. Buy your solvent cement where you buy your plastic pipe, and make *sure* it's made for the type of pipe you're using. (If it's a "universal" cement, be certain your type of pipe is listed on the container.) And don't mix different types of plastic pipe in your system. The common types are PVC (polyvinyl chloride), CPVC (chlorinated polyvinyl chloride) and ABS (acrylonitrile-butadiene-styrene). You can use any of them for drainage plumbing, but CPVC is the type widely used for water supply pipes, especially for hot water, as it can take temperatures up to about 180 degrees F. To play it safe, however, it's wise to set your water heater's thermostat control at 140 to 160 degrees F. And don't connect the plastic pipe directly to the water heater. Use foot-long lengths of metal pipe from the heater to the plastic pipe, and make the connections with suitable interconnecting fittings. This prevents the heat of the metal tank from being transferred directly to the plastic.

In all plastic pipe work, allow for expansion and contraction with temperature changes, as it's more pronounced with plastic than with metal. A 100-degree increase in temperature, for example, can add almost $3/4''$ to a 20' length of plastic pipe. So don't wedge it tightly lengthwise. The natural "give" of the plumbing system, in most cases, can more than absorb the dimensional changes.

Connecting Technique

If you're joining small pipe fittings (water-pipe size), you can use the applicator attached to the cement-can lid to apply the cement. For larger pipe, like drain and soil pipe, it's wise to use a brush, because you have to work fast. Apply the cement lightly both to the outside of the pipe on the area that will be inside the fitting and to the inside of the fitting. Then push the pipe into the fitting as far as it will go and give it a partial turn to spread the cement; then set the fitting to the exact position you have previously marked "dry." Work quickly. It's all set in about a minute. When working with large-diameter pipe, the brush width should equal about half the pipe diameter.

Read the label on the cement you use, and follow the manufacturer's precautions. A cleaner is often recommended for PVC and CPVC. This not only cleans the connecting surfaces of the pipe and fittings but also conditions them so the cement can penetrate easily. Ask about this where you buy your pipe and cement.

Flexible Plastic Pipe

Flexible plastic pipe is widely used in wells and underground pipelines from the well to the house. Common types are polyethylene and polybutylene. As these types are available in coils of 100' or more, they can be run down wells or underground with a minimum of connections, thus reducing the possibility of leaks. Their flexibility, too, makes directional changes easy. These types, however, are not connected by solvent-cementing but by clamped fittings. The rigid fitting is inserted into the flexible pipe end and clamped tightly by a stainless steel band-clamp around the outside of the pipe at the fitting location.

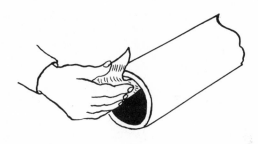

Fig. 119. After cutting use fine sandpaper to remove burrs or roughness left by the saw cut. Do not overdo the sanding, as pipe must fit snugly in fitting.

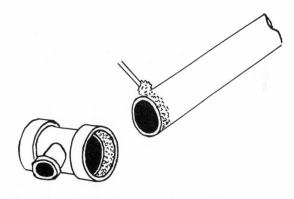

Fig. 120. Cement is applied to outside of pipe end and inside of fitting. If cleaner is required, use it before cement. Assemble connection in correct position quickly, as cement sets fast.

Fig. 121. To spread cement thoroughly, give fitting a partial turn on pipe end.

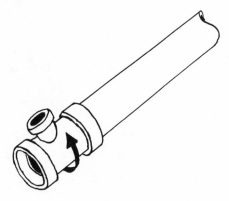

COPPER PIPE

Copper pipe may be used for both water supply and drainage plumbing, or in combination. Often, for example, copper is used for water supply pipe (both hot and cold), while plastic is used for the drainage, soil stack, etc.

In small (water supply) diameters it is usually cut with a tubing cutter, then end-reamed to remove the burr left by the cutter. It can also be hacksawed, as is done in the case of larger drainage sizes. Burrs are removed from large sizes with a file.

Fig. 122. Copper water tube can be led through joists almost as easily as cable, but make holes large enough to permit angling it in from below. A right-angle chuck attachment for your power drill helps.

Connecting Technique

Rigid copper pipe is connected by means of soldered joints. The first step, after cutting to length and reaming or file-smoothing, as above, is cleaning the pipe end. This is usually done with fine sanding cloth or sandpaper. Clean the end for a distance just slightly greater than required to enter the fitting. Rub only hard enough to remove the surface film from the pipe but not hard enough to remove the metal. (You don't want to change the diameter and produce a loose fit.)

Immediately after cleaning, apply "flux" to the cleaned portion of the pipe end and to the inside of the fitting. Buy the flux where you buy the pipe and fittings. A paste-type flux is generally preferred by do-it-yourselfers. Typically, the flux contains zinc and ammonium chlorides. Its purpose is to keep the metal surface oxide-free during the soldering process. After the flux has been applied with a small brush or clean rag, the pipe is pushed into the fitting as far as it will go. A little twist helps spread the flux.

To solder the connection, heat the fitting with a propane or butane torch, playing the flame over the fitting to heat as large an area as possible. *Do not* aim the flame into the joint between fitting and pipe. As the heat is applied, touch the solder to the joint. When it has reached soldering temperature, the solder will melt and flow into the joint by capillary action, leaving a shiny ring all the way around the pipe. Remove the torch as the solder flows in, so as not to burn the flux. The type of solder most commonly used is termed 50/50, meaning it's half lead and half tin, an easy-melting alloy. It's sold in wire form on spools where you buy copper plumbing. Any leftovers can be used for a wide variety of soldering jobs.

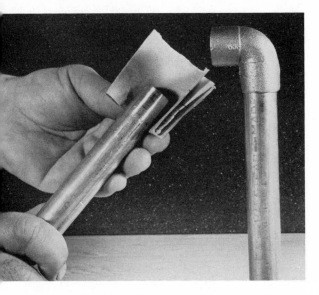

Fig. 123. If you're using copper pipe, connections are soldered. First step is cleaning pipe end with very fine sandpaper. Also clean the inside of the fitting where it will connect. But do not overdo it. Very close fit is essential between pipe and fitting. You merely want to remove oxide film. HEYMAN HARDWARE

Fig. 124. Second step is applying flux to cleaned pipe end and inside portion of fitting where pipe will fit. Flux prevents oxide formation during soldering process. Apply it with brush or wood paddle. HEYMAN HARDWARE

Fig. 125. Insert flux-coated pipe end into flux-coated fitting, and apply propane torch flame to fitting. Do not apply flame to juncture between pipe and fitting or you'll burn flux, destroying its effectiveness. Hold tip of 50/50 solder wire against juncture, like this. When fitting reaches soldering temperature, solder will flow into juncture by capillary action, making shiny ring all the way around. When it cools, pipe is permanently joined and sealed. HEYMAN HARDWARE

GALVANIZED PIPE

Galvanized steel pipe is now less commonly used by do-it-yourselfers than plastic or copper, probably because of the number of special tools required to cut and thread it. Such tools can be rented in many areas, however. Check on the availability of these tools on a rental basis if you want to use this type of pipe. The tools include a pipe vise, pipe cutter, stock and die to do the threading in the diameters you'll be using, and at least two pipe wrenches. On the job, you use one wrench to hold the pipe and the other to tighten the fitting. The tool rental agency can supply instructions for the use of the cutting and threading tools they handle.

After cutting and threading, remove any dirt or chips from the pipe end inside and out. Then apply pipe compound (like thick paint—available from plumbing suppliers) to the outside threads of the pipe *only,* never to the inside threads of the fittings. Then screw the fitting on to the piece and tighten it with the wrenches. When the joint is tight, two or three threads on the pipe will be left exposed. In measuring for overall length, you must allow for the length of the fitting and also the distance the pipe end extends into the fitting. There are fittings for connecting copper or plastic pipe to threaded steel pipe, in case your new plumbing is copper or plastic and must be connected to existing threaded pipe.

CAST IRON PIPE

This type of drainage and soil pipe is made in several forms. If your house is an older one, its soil stack and drainage plumbing is likely to be of the old "hub-and-spigot"-type cast iron pipe with "lead-and-oakum" connections. This type of connection is made by inserting the spigot (small end) of the pipe into the hub (large end) of the fitting or next section of pipe. Oakum is then packed into the space between the hub and spigot to within 3/4" of the hub rim, using a tool called a yarning iron. (Oakum is a packing and calking material made of hemp treated with tar.) The joint is then sealed with molten lead melted in a plumber's furnace or in an iron melting pot (made for the purpose) heated by a blowtorch. An iron ladle held in an insulating mitt is used to pour the lead. The ladle *must* be heated before dipping into the molten lead. The lead should be poured in a single pouring, if possible, all the way around the joint until it is even with the rim of the hub. As the lead shrinks slightly on cooling, it must be spread to form a tight joint. This is done with a chisel-like tool called a calking iron and a hammer. You tap it into the lead, working several times around the joint and calking the lead tightly against the pipe first. Then you repeat the operation, calking the lead tightly against the inside of the hub. The aim is to produce a firmly sealed joint without using so much force as to crack the hub. If the lead must be poured into a horizontal joint, a tool called a joint runner is used to act as a dam and hold the molten lead in the joint.

The chances are you won't have to undertake this type of work, though a general knowledge of the procedure will be useful in case you do. Typically, however, you might need to make only one or two connections. In this event, it might be wise to have the job done by a professional who will have the necessary tools and expertise.

NO-HUB JOINTS

A newer, more easily used form of cast iron pipe is trade-named No-Hub pipe, as it is made without the hub used in older types. The pipe end is joined to the fitting or the next length of pipe by means of a one-piece tubular neoprene gasket held by a stainless steel shield and a stainless steel retaining clamp. No lead or oakum is involved.

COMPRESSION JOINTS

Another newer form of cast iron pipe

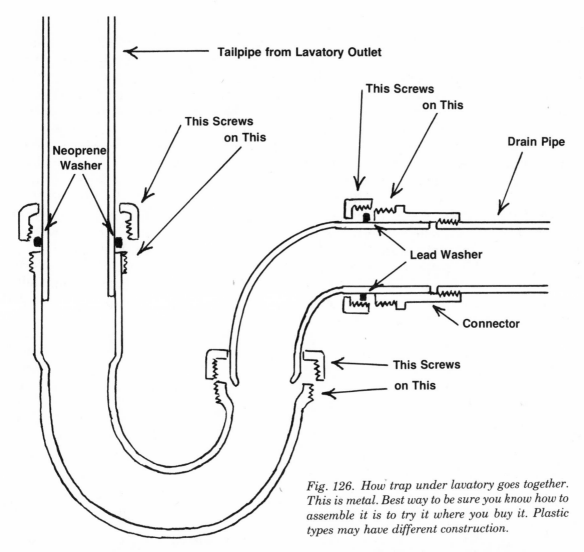

Tailpipe from Lavatory Outlet

Neoprene Washer

This Screws on This

This Screws on This

Drain Pipe

Lead Washer

Connector

This Screws on This

Fig. 126. How trap under lavatory goes together. This is metal. Best way to be sure you know how to assemble it is to try it where you buy it. Plastic types may have different construction.

joint is the compression joint used with modern hub-and-spigot-type pipe. In place of the lead and oakum between the spigot and hub, a synthetic rubber tubular gasket is used. When the spigot is forced into the hub, the gasket is compressed, forming a leakproof and pressure-proof joint. Although special tools are available to force the spigot and hub together, it can also be done by using a 2 x 4 as a lever against a stationary block and the pipe end, where space permits.

You'd be most likely to find it necessary to work with cast iron pipe in situations where an addition calls for leading the main house drain out through the foundation to the house sewer and disposal system. (In some cases, it's simpler to connect new plumbing to the existing system outside the foundation, underground.) Check your local regulations before planning any work of this type. A permit and inspection are likely to be required, in some cases also a written test in order to secure a homeowner's permit to undertake the type of work involved. In this case, obtain a copy of the local code dealing with the subject in advance.

FIXTURE CONNECTIONS

Both water supply and drainage fittings connecting to fixtures (basins, sinks, toilets, etc.) vary with the type of pipe being used and with combinations of pipe types. You might be using copper water supply pipes, for example, and plastic drains. The general details are shown in the illustrations. But buy your fixture-connecting fittings where you buy your pipe, and buy them to match your pipe and fixtures. If you encounter special fittings not covered in this chapter (new developments are frequent), inquire about the details where you buy. Some modern fittings also are designed to do things not possible with older types. You can buy plastic drainage fittings, for example, that have Twist-lock caps sealed by O-rings. These permit the positive but temporary sealing of one branch of the fitting (such as a sanitary T) for any required period of time while connecting the other branches of the fitting into the system. No cement is used. The Twist-lock cap keeps the unused branch of the fitting in like-new condition for connecting later. Just untwist the sealing cap and the fitting is ready for completion of the extra branch. This might be useful if it's necessary to put one fixture (like a sink) into operation before completing the plumbing to another (possibly a wash basin).

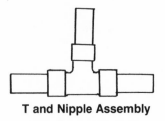

T and Nipple Assembly

Fig. 127. To tap into existing copper water tube for supply to new plumbing, first solder short lengths of copper tube into T, as below. The short lengths are often called nipples. Solder as in Figs. 123 to 125.

Fig. 128. Next, with water turned off at main valve, remove a section of water tube equal in length to T and nipple assembly from existing water supply system. Clean all pipe ends and fittings, as shown in Fig. 123, and apply flux to cleaned parts. Slide slip couplings (available from plumbing suppliers) onto cut ends of existing supply line.

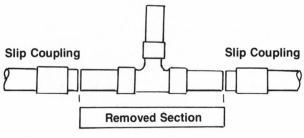

Slip Coupling   Slip Coupling

Removed Section

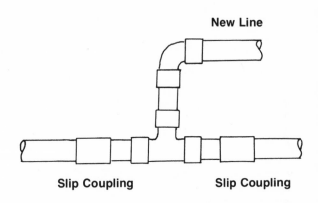

New Line

Slip Coupling   **Slip Coupling**

Fig. 129. To complete the job, place the T and nipple assembly in place of the removed section of copper pipe and move the slip couplings so their midpoints are over the junctures between the existing supply line and the T assembly. Then solder, as in Figs. 123 to 125. Clean and flux before soldering. Allow time for solder to harden, and connect new water line to third branch of T. Method is used on both hot- and cold-water lines. Similar method can be used on existing plastic lines, using appropriate plastic cement. If water lines are threaded steel pipe, threaded nipples and T make up assembly. Threaded coupling is used on one connection to old line, "union" on the other. Plumbing suppliers stock pipe unions.

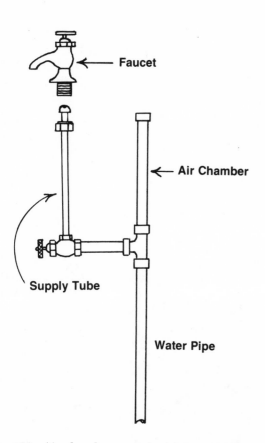

Faucet

Air Chamber

Supply Tube

Water Pipe

Fig. 130. Air chambers, required by some codes, are often used in supply lines to faucets and appliances like washing machines. Typically, chamber consists of 18″ to 24″ capped vertical section of pipe, as shown. As upper end is capped, chamber doesn't fill with water, but retains trapped air "cushion." This absorbs impact when water is turned off suddenly, and eliminates bang.

Fig. 131. Water supply plumbing for bathtub roughed in. Copper tube for faucet spout is directly above tube at center. Three parts covered by cardboard tubes, higher up, are, left, hot water valve; center, tub–shower selector valve; right, cold water valve. The valve handles will be attached after wall is covered.

ROUGHING-IN

Before you install your fixtures, you must "rough in" the water supply and drainage pipes to which they will be connected. You can do this by measuring the fixtures themselves or by referring to the owner's guide that should come with each fixture. The correct location of the pipes (especially the drain pipes) is extremely important. The "closet" connection to the outlet of a water closet, for example, must be precisely located if the flush tank is to have proper clearance from the wall behind it. If the tank must be wall mounted, equal precision is essential. Typically, the toilet drain pipe is roughed in with its center a minimum of 12″ from the finished wall behind the toilet, in order to allow space for the tank. The hole in the floor should be just large enough for the closet flange collar to drop through it with its flanged rim resting on the floor. The position of the water supply pipe to the tank will also be dimensioned on the roughing-in plan. Roughing-in measurements should also accompany tubs, sinks, shower bases and all other fixtures. To be safe, also measure the fixture itself, to make sure that the owner's guide with its roughing-in measurements is for the correct model.

It's wise, too, to provide a removable access panel in the opposite side of the wall against which the drain end of the bathtub is located. This should be of such size as to make it easy to reach the bathtub trap in case it becomes clogged. It also makes it possible to check the water supply lines to the tub for leaks that might occur later. In installations with an unfinished basement ceiling below them, the trap can be reached for cleaning from the basement if the clean-out is on the underside of the trap or if the trap is far enough below the woodwork to allow removal of a top clean-out.

Fig. 132. Source of very inexpensive fixtures is often building wrecker. Usually, fixtures such as tubs, sinks, wash basins and toilets are sold with whatever plumbing items are still attached to them, as faucets, supply lines. These, at yard of Berkshire Building Wreckers, sell for a fraction of new fixture price. PO' MAN'S PARADISE

19

HOW TO DO YOUR OWN WIRING

The mechanics of wiring your addition is merely a matter of following established rules. But before you begin, be sure you are familiar with all local regulations regarding wiring, as codes vary considerably from one locality to another. Typically, too, they require that your wiring be checked over by an inspector before it is approved for use. This inspection, in most cases, must be made before the interior wallboard is applied. Otherwise many important details would be concealed. You'll have to be sure to arrange for the inspection at an appropriate time.

THE BASICS

The wiring you'll be doing will usually involve several "branch circuits," each with its own fuse or circuit breaker. Thus an overload that blows a fuse or trips a circuit breaker shuts off the power only to the portion of the house supplied by that circuit, while the power remains "on" to the rest of the house, supplied by other branch circuits.

Most of the branch circuits in the average house (or addition) are rated at either 15 or 20 amperes (abbreviated "amps"), which means they are protected by a fuse or circuit breaker that shuts them off automatically when their electrical load reaches that amperage. The automatic shut-off devices are necessary to prevent overheating the wiring. Without such protection, wiring could become so hot (as a result of electrical overloading) that the house could be set afire.

The different amperages also require different wire sizes. In localities that follow the National Electrical Code, cable containing No. 14 wire can be used for 15-amp circuits, No. 12 wire for 20-amp circuits. (The smaller the number, the larger the wire size.)

How Many Outlets?

If you're following the national code, your receptacle outlets must be installed so that no point along the floor line of any wall in your living area rooms is more than 6' from an outlet. In kitchen and dining

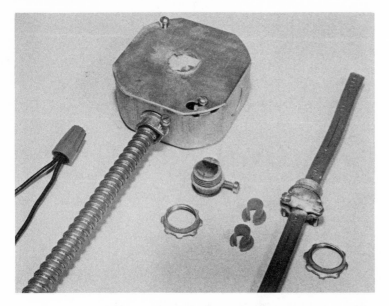

Fig. 133. Electrical materials you'll be using. Left, solderless connector holds two black wires together in electrical contact. Next, flexible armored cable (BX) leads to junction box and is held by cable clamp in knockout opening. Junction box cover can be removed by loosening screws slightly and giving cover a partial turn. To right of junction box, cable clamp and slot-rimmed nut. Threaded portion of clamp extends through box from outside, slot-rimmed nut is tightened on to it from inside, by prying with screwdriver. To right of cable clamp, plastic bushings that must be inserted into end of armored cable to prevent severed armor from cutting wire insulation. Very important: They go in before cable end goes into clamp. Right, nonmetallic sheathed cable with cable clamp tightened on it. Clamp is made to fit cable type. This one is different from BX. Slot-rimmed nut is same as for BX clamp.

areas, an outlet is also required in each counter space wider than 12″. One outlet is also required in the laundry and another in the bathroom, adjacent to the washbasin. All this, of course, results in more outlets than are to be found in many older homes, but convenience is much greater, and the hazards of trailing extension cords are largely eliminated.

How Much Electrical Capacity?

The minimum general lighting load capacity for a private house is listed in the code at 3 watts per square foot of living area, which would include your addition. Thus, an area 20′ x 50′ (which comes to 1,000 square feet) requires at least 3,000 watts lighting capacity—enough to take care of 30 bulbs of 100-watt size. To get this you'd need at least two branch circuits, and simple electrical arithmetic tells you why. As volts × amperes = watts, a 15-amp branch circuit at 120 volts can supply only 1,800 watts, a 20-amp branch circuit only 2,400 watts. So you need more than one circuit of either amperage to provide 3,000 watts. But this takes care of only your lighting and outlets for such things as radios, etc. If your addition includes a kitchen, at least two 20-amp small-appliance circuits are required for that, and another for the laundry room, if that is included. You also need additional circuits for such things as your electric range, dryer and other major appliances, if they'll be a part of your addition's equipment.

HOW TO START THE WIRING

Just how involved the wiring job will be depends to a considerable extent on the nature of your addition. If it doesn't call for appliance circuits so that all you need is wiring for general lighting, as in the case of a bedroom, it's likely to be simple enough for a beginner. In the case of a small addition like the bedroom men-

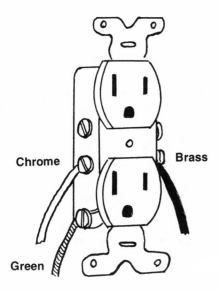

Chrome **Brass**

Green

Fig. 134. Here, only one brass terminal and one chrome terminal are used, so you can extend wiring from other two. Always connect black to brass, white to chrome.

Fig. 135. When receptacle has two black wires connected to brass terminal side and two white ones on chrome terminal side, one black and white pair leads in, the other out to next outlet. (Crosshatched wire is on grounding terminal.) You can't extend new wiring from this receptacle, as all terminals are already used and code limits number and size of wires entering each size box.

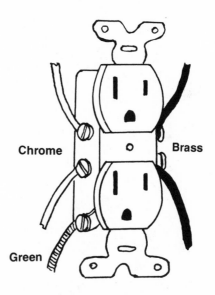

Chrome **Brass**

Green

tioned, the wiring may even start from existing circuits already in the house. In this event, the easiest starting point is a receptacle outlet at the *end* of a run of wiring in a room adjacent to the addition. To find such an outlet, shut off the current to the room either by using the main switch or by removing the fuse or turning off the circuit breaker that supplies the room. But be sure it's definitely off. (Try a lamp in each outlet you'll be examining, as some rooms are supplied by more than one fuse.) After the current is off, remove and replace the outlet cover plates one at a time and look for a receptacle that has wires connected to only two of its four terminals, as shown in the drawing. You can connect your new wiring to the two unused terminals. (Receptacles that are *not* at the end of a run have wires connected to all four terminals.) Two of the wires bring current *to* the receptacle, the other two carry it *from* the receptacle to the next one along the run.

How you lead the wiring from the end-of-run receptacle to the receptacles in your

addition depends on the situation. If there's a baseboard below the outlet, it's often possible to remove it, make a channel for the new wiring in the wallboard behind it and then replace the baseboard. In other cases, the easiest method consists of running the new wiring down through a hole bored in the floor from the basement, then on to the new addition. If an end-of-run outlet is located on an unfinished base-

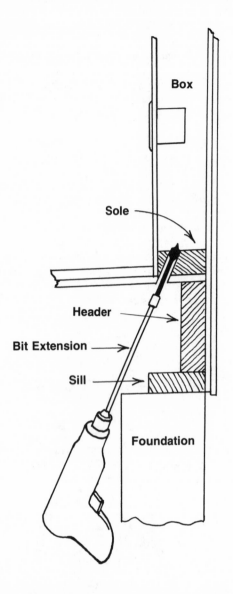

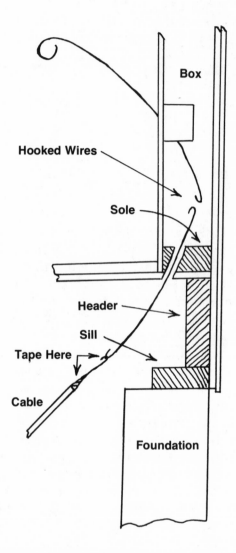

Fig. 136. *If you have to lead cable from existing box in outside wall to basement in order to extend wiring, you'll usually need a drill bit extension to clear the foundation when boring up through the subfloor and sole. Hardware stores stock the extensions to fit standard bit shanks.*

Fig. 137. *After hole is bored, remove receptacle from box (with current off), tap open knockout in bottom of box and use hooked wires to pull new cable into box. It's best if knockout opened is served by built-in clamp. Otherwise, hole through sole must be large enough to pass cable with threaded clamp already on it. Slot-rimmed nut can be applied from inside box.*

Fig. 138. Porcelain ceiling light fixture like this, often used in unfinished basements, may be a starting point for extending wiring to addition. Don't extend from it if its circuit is already heavily loaded. And don't extend from it if it is controlled by a remote switch. Switch would then shut off your new wiring when it shut off the light. Pull chain switch on light fixture is OK, as new wiring can be connected so as not to be controlled by it.

Fig. 139. Three common box types. Left, typical switch or outlet box with built-in clamps at ends, inside. Clamps can be shifted to sides if required. Box has knockouts at clamp positions, also at other locations to take threaded cable clamps shown in Fig. 133. Center, surface-mounted box. This type is not recessed in wall, but mounted on it, as might be done in workshop. Knockouts take threaded cable clamps. Right, junction box in which different runs of cable may be interconnected, as in leading wiring to different parts of house or addition.

Fig. 140. How runs of wiring can be interconnected in junction box, as when junction box is starting point for wiring to addition.

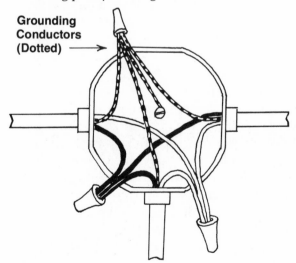

Grounding Conductors (Dotted) →

ment ceiling, it often provides the easiest starting point for wiring to other outlets in a new addition. A porcelain ceiling light fixture of the type often used in basements may also provide a starting point. These fixtures are usually mounted on a square or round box commonly called a junction box. If only one or two cables lead to the box, there's usually room for another one to lead the current to your new addition. The diagram shows typical new wiring connections inside the box. When removing box covers of any type to find possible starting points for extending wiring, *be sure the current is definitely off*. Once you've found a suitable starting point,

Fig. 141. Fuse panel, as found in many older homes. This is a small one with four plug fuses (round) and pull-out blocks for main and range fuses. The blocks are visible above the round plug fuses.

Fig. 142. Circuit-breaker panel. This is the type found in newer houses. The circuit breakers are simply reset like a snap switch when an overload on the circuit trips them. Always remove the overload before resetting a circuit breaker.

close the box and switch the current on again. Then install your new wiring, *not connected* to the starting point. When it's complete, with boxes mounted, receptacles connected and cover plates in place, *shut off the current* again and make the connections in the starting box. This way, the current need be off for only short periods during the job.

In choosing a starting point for your new wiring, be sure you're starting from a circuit that is supplying only a light load, *not* one already near its capacity. Be sure, too, to check your local code (or ask your local electrical inspector) to ascertain that what you plan to do is permissible.

If it's not feasible to start the wiring from an existing circuit (as when all existing circuits are carrying a near-capacity load), the new wiring must consist of new branch circuits starting from the fuse panel or circuit breaker panel. If you've had experience at starting new circuits in this way, you can do it yourself. If not,

don't try it. Your best bet is a professional electrician. He can start your new circuit or circuits and lead the wiring to the first outlet. You can then take it from there in the same manner as starting from an existing end-of-run outlet. It's not wise for an inexperienced person to tackle new circuit starting without specific instructions for the particular fuse panel or circuit breaker panel, as there's great variation in these units. Also, even when the main switch is off, it is possible in some types (especially older ones) to come in contact with "live" parts.

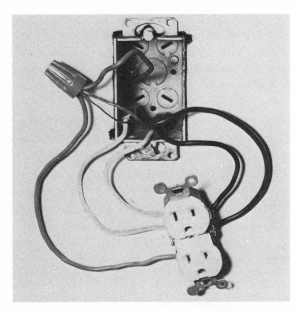

Fig. 143. Connections to outlet receptacle along the run of wiring. White wire from incoming cable connects to one chrome terminal; white wire from outgoing cable connects to other chrome terminal. Black wire from incoming cable connects to one brass terminal; black wire from outgoing cable connects to other brass terminal. Grounding conductors from both cables connect at solderless connector to wire leading to terminal in back of box and green-sprayed terminal on receptacle.

Color-keyed Wiring Makes It Easy

Once started, the wiring is made easy by the fact that the wires in your cables and the receptacle and switch terminals to which you connect them are color keyed. Typical wiring "cable" contains two power-carrying wires, one white and one black. The white wire *always* goes to the chrome terminal screws of an outlet, the black wire *always* to the brass screws. In most modern wiring leading to receptacles there's also a third wire in the cable, usually bare. This one is called the grounding conductor and is connected, as shown, to the green-sprayed terminal of the outlet. The white wire is commonly called the

"neutral" wire and the black wire the "hot" wire. They make up the two sides of the circuit so both should be considered "live." The important rule with all wiring work: *never work on wiring unless the electricity to that wiring is definitely off.*

ABOUT SWITCHES

The commonest type of switch is the single-pole snap switch that turns our lights on and off. It's also made in a quiet type for use where the usual type might be too noisy, as in sleeping areas. The two terminal screws in these switches are both brass, as switches are *always* used to

Fig. 144. Connections at wall switch if switch is in cable-supplying fixture. (Not in a switch loop.) White wire from incoming cable is connected to white wire in outgoing cable with a solderless connector. Black wire from incoming cable is connected to one switch terminal, black wire from outgoing cable is connected to the other terminal.

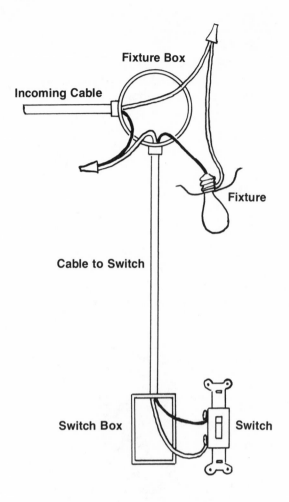

Fixture Box

Incoming Cable

Fixture

Cable to Switch

Switch Box **Switch**

Fig. 145. The only situation where black wire may be connected to white one is in switch loop. Switch that is not on incoming cable must be connected to fixture circuit with cable containing one black wire and one white wire. Connect switch so wire leading from incoming cable to it is white, and wire returning from the switch to the fixture is black. Note: fixture should always be connected so white wire leads to screw shell of bulb socket, black wire to center contact at base of socket.

"break" the black wire, *never* the white one. The only situation in which a white wire is connected to a switch is a switch "loop" where a cable must be led to a switch that is not actually in the line to the fixture being controlled by it. As cable is not made with two black wires in it, you must use cable with one black and one white. You connect the wires to the switch so that the white wire carries the current *to* the switch and the black wire carries it *from* the switch to the fixture. As the white wire in the *supply* line to the fixture runs unbroken to the fixture and is not involved with the switch, it runs to the chrome terminal. The black wire bringing current *from* the switch to the fixture connects to the brass terminal. So, although the switch must be connected to both black and white wires in the "loop" cable, the wires end up correctly connected at the fixture.

Three-way Switches

Three-way switches are often used so you can turn a light on or off from two different places, as from the top or bottom of stairs. These switches have three terminals instead of the usual two but are connected into the black wire side of the circuit as usual, though they require a 3-wire cable between them. Typically, these switches have two brass terminals and a darker, or black, one called the "common." The black wire carrying current *to* the first switch is connected to the "common" terminal. The white wire from that same cable is connected to the white wire of the 3-wire cable. At the second switch box, the other end of the cable's white wire is connected to the white wire leading to the light fixture. The other two wires in the 3-wire cable (usually a black one and a red one) run from the two brass terminals of the first switch to the two brass terminals of the second switch. Surprisingly, it doesn't matter which way they're connected. At the second switch, the black wire in the cable leading to the fixture is connected to the "common" terminal of the second switch. When the current is turned on, either switch can turn the light on or off, regardless of which switch was used last.

THE CABLES

The two common types of cable used in most house wiring are armored cable like the familiar BX cable, and nonmetallic sheathed cable like Romex. For damp places like some crawl spaces, the non-metallic cable is also made in water-resistant form. Your local code may limit you to specific types of cable inside the house. Otherwise tell your supplier whether the cable will be used in a dry or damp location, and he can recommend the proper type. If you are starting your new wiring from an existing circuit, the wires in the new cable should be the same size as those in the existing circuit. And, assuming the existing wiring contains a grounding conductor for grounded receptacles (3-prong), your new cable should also contain a grounding conductor. You buy your cable according to the size and number of wires in it, whether it has a grounding conductor and the basic type. For example 14/2 with ground type NM means the cable will contain two No. 14-size wires plus a grounding conductor, and it is nonmetallic and suited to use in dry locations. If the final letters are NMC, they indicate a water-resistant type suitable for use in damp locations as well as dry ones. Another type, designated as type UF, is so highly water resistant it may be buried in the earth for uses requiring underground wiring, as in routing power to an outbuilding. Armored cable (technically, metal-clad cable) is also widely used indoors in dry areas, especially where resistance to possible impact damage is desired. The familiar BX cable is a popular one.

Mounting the Cable

In general, cable installed in new work (such as an addition) should be supported every 4½′ and within 1′ of any box. Electrical staples may be used to support the armored cable, but metal straps (made for the purpose) should be used with non-metallic cable to avoid possible cable damage. The cables should not be bent sharply, as damage may result. The inside radius of a bend in armored cable should not be less than 7 times the diameter of type MC armored cable nor 5 times that of type AC. If you're not sure of the type, use the larger diameter.

Fig. 146. How wiring is led through walls. Simply bore holes large enough to take cable through studs easily. Boxes may be mounted directly on studs or on brackets between studs, according to required location of switch or outlet. Mount boxes carefully, allowing for wallboard thickness, so cover plate of box will be flush with wall surface.

Cutting the Cable

Nonmetallic cable is easily cut to length with large wire cutters or electricians' side cutters. It may be necessary to cut larger cables first from one side, then the other, severing one wire at a time. One of the easiest ways to cut armored cable entails bending it sharply enough so the flexible armor buckles. Then twist it slightly against the direction of the armor spiral to open the buckled strip a little farther. You can then slip metal snips between the buckled armor and the wires to cut the armor. Use the snips to trim off any sharp cut corners or edges.

Connecting the Cable to the Boxes

All electrical connections in house wiring *must* be enclosed in approved boxes. These include junction boxes that are often used simply for interconnecting runs of wiring and outlet boxes that contain receptacles or switches. The junction box may have a plain metal cover when used for interconnections only, or a cover with an outlet, switch or light fixture in it. If it has a plain metal cover, it must not be plastered over or otherwise made inaccessible. Large hardware stores and electrical suppliers stock both junction boxes (in several sizes) and standard receptacle boxes. The boxes have no openings for cable when you buy them, but have "knockouts." These are circular disks that are cut part way through the box during manufacture. Located in commonly used cable positions around the box, the knockouts are easily knocked out with hammer and metal punch (or large nail) to make cable openings wherever required. The unused knockouts remain in place so no holes remain open.

Cable clamps matched to the type of cable fit into the knockout holes and are held by large nuts inside the box. The cable is held in the clamp by tightening clamp screws on the outside. Most switch and outlet boxes have built-in clamps that are tightened on the cable from the inside, with a screwdriver.

FREEING THE WIRES

Before the cable is clamped in the box, about 8″ of its outer covering (armor or nonmetallic sheathing) must be removed to free the wires for connecting. The 8″ armor section is cut off the same way the cable was cut to length. The wires are then freed of the paper wrapping, exposing the insulating covering of the circuit wires. The grounding wire is usually bare.

The outer sheathing of plastic or other material on nonmetallic cable must be removed to free the wires. To begin, look at the cut end of the cable to see where the insulated and bare wires are located inside. You can then insert a sharp pocketknife blade so as to cut the sheathing without cutting any wire insulation. The best way to do this is to slide the knife blade along the bare conductor. After the sheathing has been slit for an inch or two, it's usually possible to grip it with pliers and roll it back along the cable to free the wires. A surface cut made in the sheathing in line with the initial slit makes the sheathing tear easily.

Baring the Wires

You will need about 8″ of wire from the inside of the cable clamps to allow length for connecting the receptacle or switch and

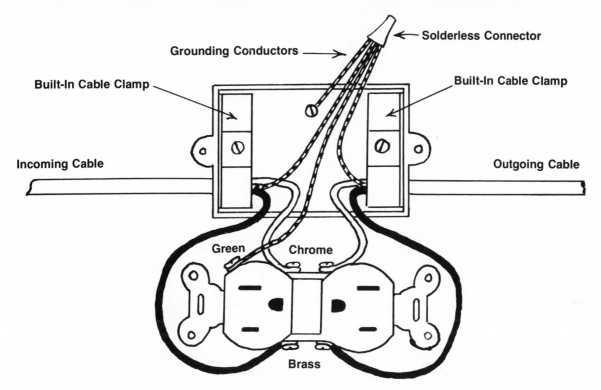

Built-In Cable Clamp

Grounding Conductors

Solderless Connector

Built-In Cable Clamp

Incoming Cable

Outgoing Cable

Green

Chrome

Brass

Fig. 147. Wire connections in outlet box. Black wires from incoming cable and outgoing cable connect to brass terminals on one side of receptacle. White wires from same cables connect to chrome terminals on other side of receptacle.

Grounding conductors (dotted) from both cables are interconnected by solderless connector to grounding conductor leading to screw in back of metal box and to green-sprayed terminal on receptacle. So, both box and receptacle are grounded.

for aligning and mounting. (After connecting the wires to the terminals, you must "fold" the wires so the receptacle or switch can be pushed into the box and fastened with the mounting screws.) To make screw terminal connections, the insulation must be removed from the ends of the wires for about $3/4''$. You do this with a pocketknife or a special insulation-removing tool available from electrical suppliers. Be careful not to nick the wire, as nicks can cause the wire to break later on. Use small-nosed pliers to form a loop in the bared end of the wire. The open gap in the loop should be about the diameter of the terminal screw. The loop should be slipped around the terminal screw so that its looped end faces in a clockwise direction. Then, as the terminal screw is tightened (clockwise) it tends to tighten the loop.

Wire-to-wire Connections

Where your wiring calls for wire-to-wire connections, as in switch and junction box work, solderless connectors are usually used. These are small, tapered plastic caps with the large end open and a conical spring lining inside the small end. To connect one or more wires together, bare their ends slightly less than the depth of the connector. Push the ends into the connector and turn it clockwise to tighten it. The conical spring lining draws the wires into the smaller end, forcing them tightly together and locking them in place. (The connector can be removed by turning it counter-clockwise.) Be sure no bared part of the wire is outside the connector, and feel the wires after tightening to be sure none are loose. The connectors are made in several sizes, to take wire diameters and combinations from lamp cord to the usual wiring sizes.

Back-wired Devices

To save time, devices such as receptacles are also made in "back-wired" form. Instead of screw terminals, they have holes in the back, labeled according to the color of the wire to be inserted. You simply push the wire into the properly labeled hole, and internal spring contacts grip and hold it firmly in place. To remove a wire, you push a narrow knife blade into an adjacent slot (often marked "push to release"), and the internal contacts release it. There's also a "strip gauge" on the back of these devices. This is a short groove into which you lay the wire end to determine the length of wire to be bared. If the bared portion doesn't extend for the full length of the groove, bare a little more. If it's longer than the groove, trim it to fit.

RACEWAY

In addition to the cable-and-box method of wiring, there's multi-outlet metal raceway, perhaps the oldest form of wiring. Although the cost of the materials may be somewhat higher with this system, the reduction in the amount of work required for a given number of outlets is surprising. You can, for example, install a dozen or more outlets in a new room by making as few as three electrical connections. And if you rearrange the room at a later date, you can rearrange your outlets as needed with relatively little work.

Essentially the commonest form of multi-outlet raceway is a hollow two-part metal channel. The back half of the channel has pre-drilled screw holes for fastening it to the wall or other surface (such as a ceiling beam), plus knockouts for cable connections. The cover section (which snaps on to the back) has rectangular openings for snap-in outlet receptacles. The receptacles are available on a pre-wired harness with spacings to match the openings in the cover. And you have a choice of spacings, from clusters as close as 4 outlets per foot to others 5 feet apart.

To install raceway, you first mount the back section along the walls of the room. The sections connect to each other with fittings that make the metal raceway into a continuous grounding conductor. And there are fittings to take it around inside and outside corners of the room wall and around vertical corners, from horizontal runs to vertical ones. There are also small, no-outlet types that look like slender moldings. These can be used to carry the wiring around the doorways and other wall openings. The raceway itself is made in forms that resemble chair moldings and baseboards.

The raceway can be started from the fuse or breaker panel or from any approved form of wiring, as in starting from a raceway adapter plate on an existing outlet box. You can also lead any approved cable into the end of the first section of raceway (with a fitting made for the purpose) or into any raceway section along the run through a knockout hole in the back section. As the outlets are pre-wired and spaced along the wiring to match the spacing of the outlet openings in the raceway cover, all you need do electrically is connect the wires from the string of raceway outlets to the wires of the cable that will provide the power, and most of the job is

Fig. 148. Raceway. Look carefully at the back wall just above the workbench and you'll see an example of Wiremold multi-outlet raceway. The little black rectangles are outlets at 12" spacing.

The same raceway is made with outlet spacings up to 5', for use throughout house. Connections at end of raceway activate all outlets along it. THE WIREMOLD COMPANY

done. The wire in the raceway outlet strings is No. 12, so your lead-in cable should have the same size wire. Connectors made for the raceway enable you to make connections in seconds. Once the outlet wiring is connected, you simply snap the outlets into the openings in the raceway cover and then snap the cover on to the back section already mounted on the wall. And that introduces a special raceway advantage. You install raceway *after* the wall is covered with wallboard, not before it's covered. So you can do the job even after you've moved your furniture into the room and have some idea where you'd like your outlets. (Blank cover sections that cost less can be used where outlets aren't needed.) Later on, if you want to change the arrangement, you simply pry off the covers, disconnect the outlet wiring, shift it where you want it, reconnect it, and snap the covers back accordingly. Naturally, this has to be done with the power *off*. The covers are made so that two screwdrivers and adult strength are required for removal. Children can't get them off.

You use a hacksaw to cut the raceway to fit the walls. The fittings for corners and other direction changes will fit the cut ends. Your best bet, if you'd like to use raceway, is your local electrical supplier. If he doesn't stock a particular fitting that you'll need, he can order it. If you use Wiremold raceway (shown in the illustrations), all fittings come with complete instructions for use. (The address of the Wiremold Company is listed at the end of this book.)

ABOUT GFI's

Outdoor electrical outlet receptacles (as on an outside wall) and those in bathrooms must be protected by ground fault circuit interrupters, usually called "GFI's." These electronic devices, connected into the house wiring, instantly shut off the power if there is a fault current (leakage) to ground. Such current leakage might occur if you were touching a defective appliance or power tool while standing on a damp basement floor, or while you were in contact with a grounded object like a faucet. The leakage current then passes through you to the ground. It can occur in many other ways, too.

The danger is in the fact that a very slight current leakage of this type may be far too small to blow a fuse or trip a circuit breaker yet still can kill a person. You can be electrocuted, for example, by as little as $60/1000$ of an ampere passing through your chest, as might happen if the current traveled from one hand to the other. Yet that amount of current, barely enough to light a $7\frac{1}{2}$-watt Christmas tree bulb, is far too little to blow a fuse. A typical GFI, however, can detect a fault current of little more than $5/1000$ of an ampere (5 milliamperes) and shut off the power in as little as $25/1000$ of a second. The timing is important, as a current as low as 60 milliamperes can stop the heart from beating in one second. So, not surprisingly, the National Electrical Code now requires them, as mentioned above, in new wiring. The GFI protects you only against ground fault situations, however, not against line-to-line contact, as in touching both a hot wire and a neutral one.

Electrical suppliers stock GFI's in numerous forms. Some can simply be installed in the outlet box itself, where they serve as both a receptacle and a GFI.

Fig. 149. Ground fault interrupter (GFI). This device, now required by code for all outdoor outlets and bathroom outlets, shuts off current when there is a current leakage to ground. Such leakage, often potentially capable of causing fatal shock, might result from insulation breakdown in tool or appliance, or from 110-volt radio falling into bathtub or pool. Other GFI types fit into outlet boxes, also replace circuit breakers. Portable GFI units are available, too. Plug the portable unit into outlet and plug tool or appliance into the unit. HARVEY HUBBELL, INC.

Others are designed to be installed in place of a circuit breaker and to serve both as a GFI and a circuit breaker. Be sure to get the wiring instructions for the ones you buy. If you'd like to add one quickly in existing wiring, a portable type is also made by the Wiring Device Division of Harvey Hubbell, Inc., Bridgeport, Conn. 06602. You simply plug the GFI into a grounded outlet and plug your tool or appliance cord into the GFI.

VII

Patios, Porches and Decks

20

PATIOS AND PORCHES

A patio, porch or deck can expand your home's living area faster than most projects that you can dream of.

THE QUICKEST

Quickest, easiest and cheapest is the crushed stone patio or terrace. It has more than time and price going for it—it is attractive, adaptable to decorative planting and expandable. And it can also be used as a base for more expensive surfacing later.

When ordering crushed stone for a patio or terrace, specify what you want it for, as crushed stone is available in several sizes. Be sure you order the right size for your particular project. Half-inch size is ideal for patios and walkways, being comfortable to walk on and not rough on shoe heels, and it compacts enough so that the legs of chairs and tables remain level.

The first step is to remove the sod from the area with a shovel or spade. This material can be saved for filling in bare spots in the lawn or for extending the lawn itself. Next, cover the desodded area with roofing felt. This will prevent grass and weeds

from cropping up through the crushed stone. Another bonus when using the roofing felt—you can trim to an exact size and shape, and from there estimate the amount of material you will need for the finished job. A 2″ layer of sand over the roofing felt

Fig. 150. Easy patio surfacing with sparkle. Marble chips are sold in bags by mason suppliers. These bags weigh 60 lbs., not too difficult to handle. Follow instructions given in text for crushed stone.

Fig. 151. For terraces not graded around trees, this arrangement stops most weeds from growing through surface, makes leveling patio blocks, bricks or flagging easier.

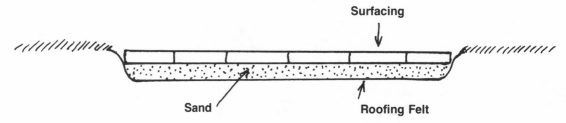

Surfacing

Sand

Roofing Felt

Fig. 152. Here, sloping lawn has been leveled with sand banked up inside loose stone perimeter wall, in preparation for marble chip surface layer. Wheelbarrow or garden cart is essential if sand must be transported from truck-delivered pile. Bags of chips can be carried in same way. Creeper-covered stump at left was later cut off close to grade line and burned to ground level, using kerosene.

can be leveled more easily than soil to make an even base for the crushed stone. If your terrace area is located so that the truck delivering the crushed stone can drive over the patio without traveling over any part of your septic system (if you have one) or drainage tiles of any kind, you are in luck. A skillful driver can spread an even layer of stone directly from the truck so that all you have to do is smooth out a few small bumps and even out around the edges. However, if this is not possible, and the stone must be unloaded some distance from the patio site, use any leftover roofing you have. Cover the grass so the stone pile does not create a problem on an established lawn area. Take small loads in a wheelbarrow or garden cart to the patio. A helper to spread each barrow-load as it arrives speeds the work. It is a good idea

Fig. 153. Chip-surfaced terrace was completed in a weekend for slightly more than cost of deck chairs and table.

for the workers to switch jobs as the work progresses—it minimizes muscle aches the next day! An iron rake used upside down is ideal for leveling both the sand and the stone. Remove and roll up the roofing from the stone pile site as soon as the job is done and save it for another day. If allowed to stay on your lawn area, it will kill your grass.

PATIO BLOCKS

These are an excellent choice for a smooth-surfaced terrace or patio. Available in many shapes and sizes, they may be used in conjunction with crushed stone and planted areas. They also lend themselves to paths and walkways. The same base used for a crushed stone terrace is used for patio block. The leveling of the sand base is more important, as the blocks can make an

Fig. 154. Standard 8" x 16" patio blocks at mason suppliers' yard. They're usually more expensive if you have them truck-delivered than if you pick them up by car. They vary in weight according to thickness, usually either $1\frac{1}{2}$" or 2". Keep your car loads within maximum passenger weight car can carry. Large terrace or patio may require several trips to mason supplier.

Fig. 155. Patio block shapes available vary with supplier. These range from concrete brick sizes, left, to Spanish tile and hexagonal forms. Important: Colors deepen when blocks are wet, as shown by stacks at rear, sun dried at top, still rain soaked below. Plan color effect on dry basis.

Fig. 157. Round paving blocks like these, often called "bubble stones," are often used for decorative effect here and there in large areas of gravel or marble chips. They're available in a variety of sizes at large mason supply outlets.

Fig. 156. Scallop-edged block at left is used vertically (scallops up) to trim patio or terrace where required, as where one side of area must be recessed in ground for leveling. Spanish tile shape is designed so tiles fit together like jigsaw puzzle. Half blocks are available to provide straight edge at perimeter of paved area. Hexagonal blocks are easy to lay. Half blocks also available for straight perimeter. Square blocks (16" on a side) can be used in contrasting colors for checkerboard effect.

uneven surface unless they are flush with each other. However, if you don't rush the job, all will be well, and corrections can be made as the work progresses. A mason's level is a help, but if you don't have one, an inexpensive line level stretched across the patio area will serve your purpose. Plan your terrace so it has a slight slope away from the house for rain runoff. About $1/4"$ downslope for every 2' is enough. Use a small garden trowel to shift the base sand around under the blocks, and allow about $1/8"$ between the blocks. Any excess sand should be brushed out over the entire surface to fill the crevices between the blocks.

Patio blocks can be laid in any number of patterns, and don't be fooled by the term "blocks." They are actually "paving blocks," typically $1^1/_2"$ or 2" thick, and are available in a wide variety of sizes and shapes. These include the usual 8" x 16",

the less common 16″ x 16″ and round "bubble stones" in a size range to enable you to design almost any style patio and garden combination you desire. There are also Spanish tile patterns. You may have to shop around for the size or shape you want, however, as many mason suppliers stock only the rectangular 8″ x 16″. All can be edged with special shapes to finish off the patio area and to make an even edge that is easy to maintain where it meets the lawn or garden. A wide range of "built-in" colors is available, including natural, rose, charcoal, green and yellow. A trip to your masonry supplier before you begin your project will be a great help in designing your patio.

Fig. 159. Terrace in Fig. 153 surfaced with 8″ x 16″ patio blocks. Sand and chips served as base for blocks, made leveling easy. Block paving job was done in less than a day. Marble chips were left in areas where plantings are located in terrace. Combination of surface materials produces attractive two-tone effect.

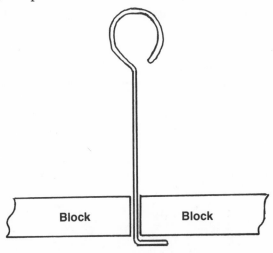

Fig. 158. Use heavy galvanized wire or bicycle spoke to make this block lifter in case you ever need to lift patio block from mid area of terrace, as for re-leveling. Push L-bend down between blocks and turn it so L hooks under block, then pull up.

Fig. 160. Night view of terrace shown in Fig. 159. Oil lamp lights table. Yellow bug bulb (bugs are not attracted to it) in coach lamp on house wall provides quick illumination without attracting mosquitoes. Torches add atmosphere, also have considerable effect as insect repellents and destroyers. (You can see numerous insects fly into flame.) See Figs. 198 to 201 for oil lamp details.

Fig. 161. *Clustered shade tree flourishes in porous gravel area provided in patio-block-paved terrace ten years after terrace was completed. Water and air can reach tree roots near surface, an essential to survival of many species.*

Fig. 162. *If your terrace or patio must be on the south side of the house, use evergreens and awning for complete shade. This one is paved with patio blocks.*

NATURAL PAVING STONES

These natural materials like slate and flagstone, while costing considerably more than patio blocks, lend themselves to attractive effects in terraces, steps and stepping-stones. Also, they can be laid directly on the turf, with spacing to allow the grass to grow between the individual flags. Since the flags are not as thick as the patio blocks, the area can be mowed to keep the grass outlines neat and trim. However, you can also use the roll-roofing layer, as with crushed stone or patio blocks, and forget the mowing chore. Just brush sand into the crevices between the flagstones. The natural paving materials available depend on your home location, though there are generally two or more types from which to choose. Among the most widely available are bluestone and slate. The latter can be bought in several colors, most often red

Fig. 163. *Rectangular cut bluestone, often used for flagging. Compare price with that of same material in random shapes. Use sizes you can handle. Weight is important, especially if you do the laying without help.*

and gray. You can use a single color or a combination. Several thicknesses are also usually stocked by mason's suppliers. Typically, natural paving materials are sold by the pound in cut rectangles or in random shapes that are somewhat more difficult to fit together, but suited to a natural setting. And they're usually less expensive than the rectangles for a given area.

If you're fortunate enough to live in a marble-producing region, where marble is often available at lower than usual cost, you can use that lovely material for a terrace with a definite touch of lavishness. You can select from many types and colors.

From the decorative standpoint, whatever natural paving material you use lends

Fig. 164. Here, shallow porch is extended with large awning and flagstone floor, rimmed with concrete wall. For choice of wall facings see Fig. 165.

Fig. 165. If your terrace is graded high enough to require a retaining wall, look at your mason supplier's selection of stone facing types. This is a display at a Plasticrete outlet.

Patios and Porches 147

Fig. 166. *If there's a valued shade tree where you'd like to build a sheltered terrace, build around it. Here, a large pin oak rises through the shade-framing that tops a flagstone terrace which includes well space around the tree trunk. Important: If you grade up around a tree in building a terrace, use porous fill like crushed stone to admit water and air needed by the tree. Tightly packed fill can kill the tree.*

Fig. 167. *From the front, tree appears to be growing out of the house.*

itself well to an eye-pleasing effect. And if price is not a factor, you can use the natural paving stone as a surfacing on a poured concrete patio. Lay it in mortar. The various stone colors against nature's backdrop of soft greens and browns allow you to use the whole gamut of colors in your garden when it comes to furnishing your outdoor living space. Match your flower colors to your cushions on seating benches and tablecloths for a total look.

BRICKS

These lend themselves to patio and terrace construction in many ways. They can be laid in sand and in many patterns from plain edge-to-edge to more sophisticated designs. The only limits to your brick designs are your own imagination and the style of your home. As bricks are small and lightweight, handling them is an easy job—even children can be allowed to help in this kind of project. And as they will be using the patio, helping to build it gives them a feeling of sharing in the enterprise and at the same time teaches them one of the basics of building and doing-it-yourself, which can be a lifetime bonus. The one who can do it is always ahead of the game.

As shown in the diagrams, brick can be used to suit your own plan. There is one precaution: when you are using brick for a terrace or walk, be *sure* you are using brick that can withstand winter freeze in your area. (Grade SW has a high degree of frost resistance.) To be sure, check with your local supplier, telling him what you want the brick for.

Fig. 168. Brick laid in sand surfaces this terrace adjoining kitchen and driveway. On east side of house, it's sunny in morning, shady in afternoon.

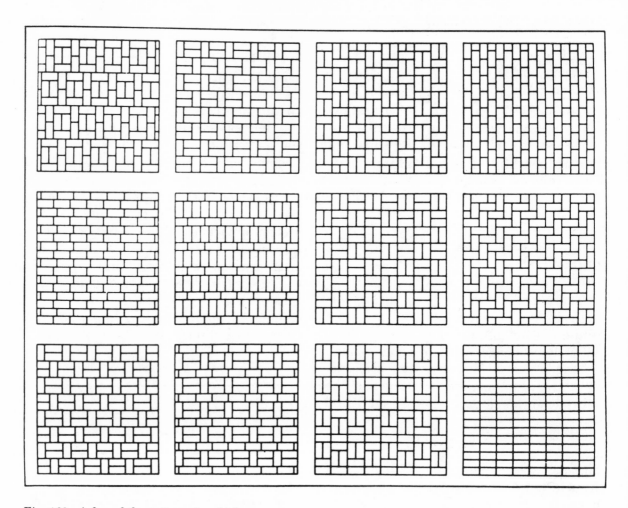

Fig. 169. A few of the patterns in which you can lay brick or rectangular block. BRICK INSTITUTE OF AMERICA

A CONCRETE PATIO OR TERRACE

This can not only be a charming addition to your outdoor living space, it can also be a base for a porch or a new room to be added to your home when the budget permits. When this is your long-range plan, have the slab thick enough (top surface high enough off the ground) so that when the superstructure is finished, snow and rain won't soak into the sill seal, caus-

ing dry rot. A low masonry block wall, rimming the slab, may also be added before the framing begins. In some areas the concrete patio or terrace will add to your taxes simply because it *may* become a part of a new addition. In others it can go for years simply as a terrace. This is another point to check out with your local zoning and building boards. A concrete terrace also eases the yearly chore of clearing it of leaves and other debris—there are no cracks and crevices to clean out, and snow removal is a breeze.

When you decide that the concrete terrace space might be put to better use as an enclosed room, you have the base at hand. Also, the exterior door you used when stepping out onto the concrete terrace can be used as an entry to the newly enclosed room, or, in the event the enclosed area requires an egress to the outside, the original exterior door can be re-used for that purpose and a less expensive interior door purchased for the entrance to your new room from the house. It always pays to consider and reconsider the uses of the materials you have at hand. When you plan to convert a concrete patio to a room at a later date, build your forms so that it can be poured as a single slab. In any case, you will need forms to contain the concrete, which should be about 4″ thick except in extremely cold areas. Stock 2 x 4's can be used to make the forms. The 2 x 4's should be set on edge and nailed to stakes at about 4′ intervals. If your patio will be subject to frost in winter, air-entrained concrete, which contains a chemical that forms millions of tiny bubbles, has a built-in resistance to this type of damage. Another method is to embed metal mesh in the concrete. Then, in the event of frost heave, the mesh will prevent the slab from separating at any crack that may occur. (Masonry suppliers sell the mesh.)

When your concrete patio is to remain a patio, you can do the job yourself, especially when you like the appearance of wood grids to make a pattern, or set off areas for plantings, barbecues or play areas for little people. The grids make it easy for you to do the pouring yourself. When grids are to be a permanent part of a concrete patio, they should be redwood or rot-proofed lumber.

A porch or other enclosed room can be built on the base provided by a concrete patio or terrace. Use a carbide-tipped drill where the sill will be, and drill matching holes in the sill members. Use fiberglass sill seal between the wood and masonry. Threaded rod is then used, with a generous epoxy coating on the rods, to anchor your sill to the base. Use a hacksaw to cut the rods off above the surface of the wood of the sill. From there on, follow the method described in the chapters on how to build floors, walls and roofs.

Ready-mixed Material

When you are using dry-mixed material, your garden cart or wheelbarrow can serve as a mortar bed. After blending the dry ingredients, add the water called for. The directions on the sacks of the ready-mixed cement are a sure guide, but after doing some of this work you will soon find the proportion of dry material to water that is easiest to work with for the particular job you are doing. Experience will tell you how much area and at what depth a sack will cover. Dry-mixed concrete, sold in sacks, varies in weight from one brand to another. Typically, two 80 lb. bags will make a 2′ square, theoretically 4½″ thick, but count on 4″ to allow for shrinkage and spillage. This is helpful when designing your gridwork and in planning your time schedule. After each grid is filled, it should be screeded level with the grid. A screed board is usually a straight 2 x 4 on edge, and you need a helper. The board is moved gently from side to side across the freshly poured concrete, which will be quite uneven in appearance. As the screed board progresses across the surface, it smooths and levels. Once the concrete has set, sprinkle it with water for a few days, as moist-curing strengthens it. If the patio is subjected to hot sun, a covering of hay or plastic to hold the moisture will prevent too rapid drying out.

If the patio is to be a large one and located so that a ready-mix truck cannot reach it because of a septic system in its path, as mentioned in the discussion of crushed stone, it will pay to purchase your material from a mason's supply yard and to rent a cement mixer from a tool rental company. You can locate one by looking in the Yellow Pages of your phone directory. Recommended proportions for making a patio are 1 sack portland cement to $2\frac{1}{4}$ cubic feet of sand, 3 cubic feet of crushed stone in $\frac{1}{2}''$ size and 5 gallons of water. (For measuring, your best bet is to make a square wooden box with inside dimensions of 1 cubic foot.) The cement comes in 94 lb.

bags, containing one cubic foot. The sand and crushed stone are available at the same yard where you get your cement and are sold by the cubic yard. Again it is a good idea to have some material to receive the sand and stone if it has to be dumped on a lawn area, to make for easy clean-up when the job is completed. In the event the material must remain on the lawn, a light raking and re-seeding may be necessary, but at least you won't have to contend with a sandy layer or ground-in stone that can damage your mower.

All poured patios and terraces should have a slope of $\frac{1}{4}''$ to the foot away from the house to provide for water runoff. Without this slight pitch, water can be pocketed against the house wall—an invitation to dampness. The $\frac{1}{4}''$ pitch is so slight that it doesn't show and will not interfere with furniture or activities.

21

DECKS

Deck construction also follows the same general framing procedure as in building a house floor. The platform, however, is usually floored with 2 x 4's or 2 x 6's with a $1/4''$ gap between them. A scrap of $1/4''$ plywood, with a nail through it (to keep it from falling down between the boards), makes a convenient spacer. Footings must conform to your local code. If there is no code in your area, a simple footing can be made by digging a hole about 18″ or 20″ square to a depth below the frost line. Fill the hole with concrete, and embed a bracket (or a bolt, head down) to anchor the supporting posts of the deck perimeter. At the house side, a header is nailed directly to the house wall into the studding, or you can use lag screws. The joist size will depend on the span of your deck. If you have a code, follow it, of course. Where there is no code, use a size that matches those in your house. You can see and measure those in your cellar or crawl space. When you match the sizes you can safely enclose the deck at a later date, should you need an enclosed room. However, if you do not plan on enclosing it, you can save time, work and money by using 2′ spacing between

the joists, rather than the 16″ used in house construction. This is often done, as the deck does not have to support the usual house load.

Fig. 170. First step in deck construction, concrete footings for the supporting posts. These have been poured into holes slightly below frostline depth. Wood boxes above surface are forms for upper portion. Deck will replace small back porch at right.

Fig. 171. When wood boxes are removed after concrete hardens, footing looks like this with post on it. Metal rod embedded in concrete extends 6" up into hole in lower end of post.

Fig. 172. Deck framing partially completed on post supports.

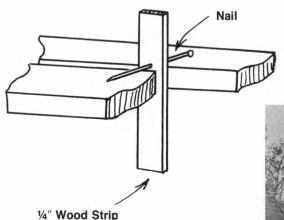

Nail

¼" Wood Strip

Fig. 173. Simple tool for spacing gaps between deck flooring boards. Drive a finishing nail through ¼" thick wood strip, slip it between boards, and push boards together. Finishing nail keeps strip from falling through. Use two of these tools about 4' apart to get even spacing.

Fig. 174. Deck with floor boards, railings and steps in place. Note that section at right has joists at house frame spacing, as enclosed room is being built on it. Space beneath is enclosed for storage.

RAILINGS

Railings for decks should be at such a height that they protect adults and children from tumbling to the lawn below when the deck is used for fun and games, as well as the usual family cook-out. This is especially necessary when the deck is a high riser, such as one that is available from the living area of a raised ranch. When such a deck can also be reached from lawn level, railings should be installed for stairway safety to the deck level. Safety gates can be added as well.

Fig. 175. Completed deck, looking from left end toward completed dining room at right end. Sliding doors from dining room provide access.

Fig. 176. This deck serves usual outdoor living purposes and doubles as a play area for small children. Close-spaced pickets instead of open railing keep small fry safe and in sight from kitchen windows. Outside stairs won't be added until children are older.

Fig. 177. Pulley clothesline easily used from deck
in Fig. 176.

Fig. 178. Oriental railing pattern made from 2 x 4
lumber.

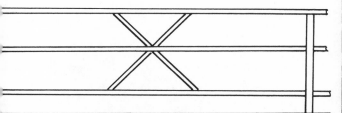

Fig. 179. Central X railing pattern.

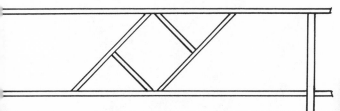

Fig. 180. Offset rectangle pattern.

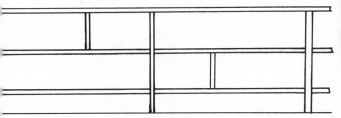

Fig. 181. Tipped square design.

Fig. 182. In snow areas, tilted top rail of railing sheds snow quickly in winter, prevents rail puddling in summer.

Fig. 183. Small "dinner" or sun decks can be built in a weekend or two, as a family project. Here, masonry blocks (hollow cores later filled with concrete) were used to build piers and pilasters (against house foundation) in holes dug below frost line. Joists and headers are 2 x 8, decking is 2 x 6. (For general construction details of small- to average-size decks, see Fig. 188.)

Fig. 184. Completed deck is low-cost outdoor dining area in evening, also sunbathing spot during morning hours. Overall size: 10' x 10'.

Fig. 185. Railed, tree-shaded deck built by same method as preceding one. Area of this one is $10^{1}/_{2}'$ x 20'.

Fig. 186. Breakfast deck built as part of bedroom addition. Sliding doors lead to bedroom. Here, temporary props hold it up while concrete sets in self-leveling footing extension shown in Fig. 187.

Fig. 187. Footing extension detail. (See Fig. 186). Footing was poured in dug hole. After it hardened, half-gallon motor oil cans with both ends removed were used instead of wooden boxes to extend piers above ground. Cans were filled with concrete up to level of post bottom. Cans may be left to rust away, or removed with can opener of rocker type.

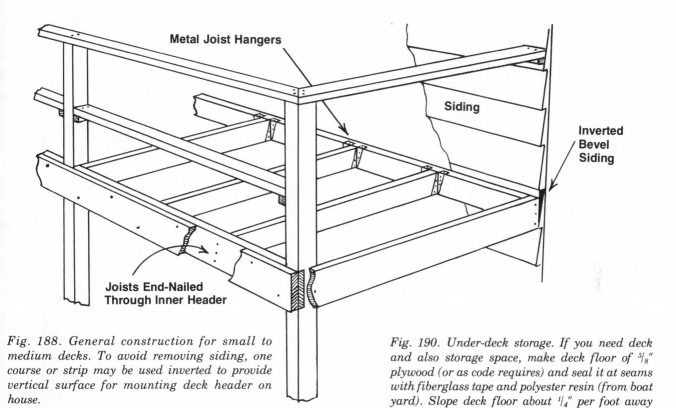

Metal Joist Hangers

Siding

Inverted Bevel Siding

Joists End-Nailed Through Inner Header

Fig. 188. General construction for small to medium decks. To avoid removing siding, one course or strip may be used inverted to provide vertical surface for mounting deck header on house.

Fig. 189. Corner construction of deck. Note the nailing pattern.

Fig. 190. Under-deck storage. If you need deck and also storage space, make deck floor of $5/8$" plywood (or as code requires) and seal it at seams with fiberglass tape and polyester resin (from boat yard). Slope deck floor about $1/4$" per foot away from house. You can then enclose space below with plywood and provide entrance door. Stop plywood above ground, and close intervening space with aluminum flashing, lower edge embedded in ground.

Fig. 191. Another example of under-deck storage. Here, plywood is shingled to match house. Windows in storage space minimize mold and mildew, permit storage of summer furniture and pool accessories.

Fig. 192. Safety system. You can locate aboveground swimming pool so only access to it is from deck built on house, like this one. Small children can't get into pool.

Fig. 193. Another possibility if you're planning an enclosed porch. This is one supported by telephone poles, cut to length. Check with your local phone or utility company on availability of old poles, often free.

Fig. 194. This enclosed, insulated porch, now a formal dining room, was originally an open deck. Deck boards were covered with $\frac{1}{2}$" plywood and carpeting. Railings were replaced with wall construction and shed roof as in chapters 15 and 16. Insulation was installed between floor joists and covered with $\frac{1}{4}$" plywood. Space under porch serves as sheltered terrace for cookouts. Posts are 4 x 6 fir.

Fig. 195. Bi-level deck like this can have section for lounging and sunning, another for dining. U.S. PLYWOOD CO.

Fig. 197. If you want deck that's soft underfoot, use indoor-outdoor carpet. Bring it indoors after drying for winter storage for maximum service life. ARMSTRONG CORK CO.

Fig. 196. Portion of deck that adjoins house is built like ordinary single-level deck. Inner ends of joists are supported by joist hangers; outer ends are supported by nails through inner member of doubled header. Header-supporting posts are 4 x 6. Lower, outer portion of deck has joists supported at inner ends by joist hangers on outer member of header. Outer ends are supported by nails, as described earlier.

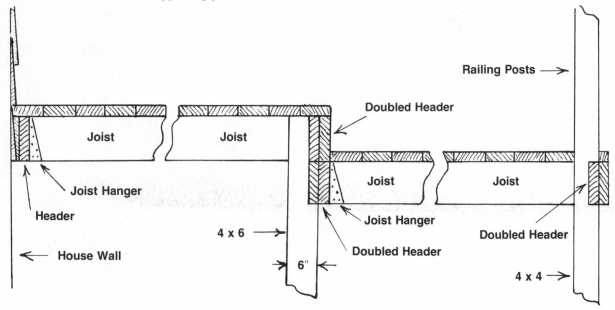

Outdoor Lighting—Without Electricity

Fig. 198. Non-electric outdoor lighting. Left to right: kerosene lantern, tubular wick oil lamp (available with or without light-increasing "mantle"), common flat wick oil lamp. Lantern serves best as guide or marker light. Tubular wick lamp provides ample illumination, especially with light-increasing mantle (a special mesh tube above wick), but costs more than conventional flat wick lamp. Flat wick lamp is most widely used type, provides adequate light when used as table lamp. Also serves well indoors in event of power outage. Advantage of oil lamps: mellow light, portability, all-night operation on one filling.

Fig. 199. To light conventional kerosene lanterns, press lever down to lift glass and chimney, then light wick. Lift lever up to lower glass and chimney, and adjust wick by turning adjusting wheel until flame is bright and smoke-free. To turn it out, press lifting lever down and blow under glass to extinguish flame.

Fig. 200. To light flat wick oil lamp, lift off chimney and turn wick up enough to permit lighting with match. Then turn wick down about flush with top of slot in metal flame spreader, and replace chimney. Adjust again to get bright smoke-free flame. To turn lamp out, blow in top of glass chimney. Same applies to mantle types.

Fig. 201. Patio torch. To light torch simply remove wick cap from top (don't remove entire lid) and light with match. To extinguish flame replace cap over wick. Keep your fingers clear of flame.

VIII

Popular Ways to
Enlarge Your House

22

GATHERING IDEAS

The steps in the construction of four distinctly different types of add-ons to homes of current design are shown in the following pages—along with their floor plans. The existing sections of the houses to which the new space was added are indicated by double-lined walls. The new portions are indicated by black walls.

As home designs vary widely in form and dimension, these examples are intended mainly to show typical possibilities and to demonstrate the fact that the average homeowner can do much of the building work himself, with professional help if it's needed. Most of the work on the additions illustrated was done by the homeowners, in some cases as a family project.

In each instance, the additions were thought about and discussed well in advance, often with resulting changes in the early planning stages—a point to remember when you begin planning an addition of your own. The object, of course, is to build to suit your needs, to do it at a price you can afford and within the time you can spare for the work you do on it.

As you look at the pictures of the individual additions, note that the methods vary somewhat with the builder, whether amateur or professional. Sometimes changes result from unexpected circumstances. Be ready to take it in stride. A new approach may be necessary because of uncontrollable factors like the weather. A premature frigid spell plus an early snowstorm played a part in one of the examples. But the work was completed without much delay.

The pictures tell the story. And the construction details in earlier chapters show how it all goes together. Only the real thing can tell you more. Keep that in mind! If you see some new construction under way, amble in and watch it for a while. In case you're not quite sure you can do it, actually seeing it done may give you the nerve to try it yourself. It often happens.

23

ADDING A TWO-CAR GARAGE
AND GAINING A FAMILY ROOM

Two problems were solved by this addition. First, shelter was provided for the second car that previously had remained in the driveway on cold winter nights and often called for tedious early-morning windshield scraping after a nighttime sleet storm. Second, the original one-car basement garage became a large family room and permitted the old, undersized one to serve as a cozy den.

Only moderate excavation by a bulldozer (hired with operator) was necessary to provide a level base for the new garage in the sloping lawn. A somewhat unusual feature of the construction is the direction of the ceiling joists, which run parallel to the ridge of the roof. The girder runs from the front to the back of the garage, between the two sides. This arrangement was chosen to provide as much space above the cars as possible so cars could be run up on ramps for repairs and hoods could be opened fully at the same time. The girder between the two sides of the garage was no obstruction. It was mounted at front and rear with anchor bolts to act as a tie beam between walls.

The original blacktop driveway, no longer needed in front of the family room picture window, was bulldozed and carted away. A temporary crushed stone driveway served the new garage for a season, then provided the base for a new blacktop one.

Fig. 202. Before. House is popular design with single garage built under bedroom wing.

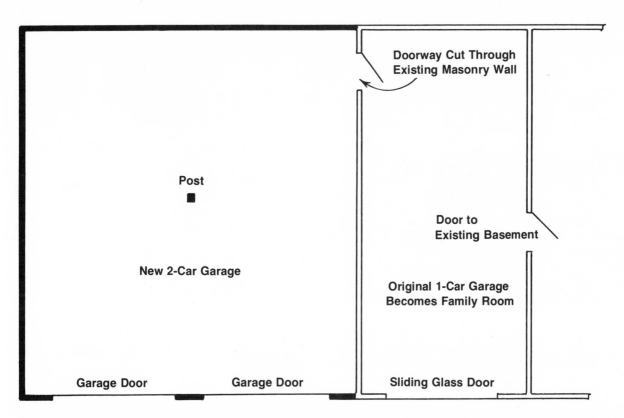

Post

New 2-Car Garage

Doorway Cut Through
Existing Masonry Wall

Door to
Existing Basement

**Original 1-Car Garage
Becomes Family Room**

Garage Door   **Garage Door**   **Sliding Glass Door**

Fig. 203. Two-car garage 24' square was added beyond outer wall of original 12' x 24' garage. Original garage became family room. Hammer drill was rented to bore through old foundation wall in series of closely spaced holes, later broken through for doorway to new garage.

Fig. 204. After. With two-car garage added, old built-in garage becomes family room with sliding glass doors in place of old garage door. Old door is one of two in new garage. Old blacktop driveway and new one, temporarily crushed stone, are both visible here.

Adding a Two-car Garage and Gaining a Family Room   167

Fig. 205. First step. Ground next to house was leveled, and foundation for new garage built of masonry block. Shingles have been removed from house where front and back walls will attach, also in center, where full-height post to ridge board is erected. Not always done, this establishes roof peak and pitch in advance.

Fig. 206. Wall framing is erected on top of foundation walls. Shingles have been removed from house wall to height of new garage ceiling joists. Grass still grows in front of garage door opening.

Fig. 207. Outer garage gable wall framing is erected with braced support for ridge board at center.

Fig. 208. Garage roof rafters are mounted. This shows upper rafter ends nailed to ridge board, house-end rafter nailed to house sheathing after removal of shingles.

Fig. 209. Outer ends of rafters notched to seat on sill with overhang protruding.

Fig. 210. All roof rafters in place, homeowner measures gable end for studs that will run from plate to rafters.

Fig. 211. Studding in gable end is complete (note that centerpost bracing remains) and plywood sheathing has been applied to end wall up to plate. Plywood roof decking has begun, starting from lower ends of rafters.

Fig. 212. Inside partially completed garage, rear roof decking provides shelter for family car. Post supports fore-and-aft girder under ceiling joists that run between gable ends. Joist direction was chosen for extra height above cars, uninterrupted by crosswise girder.

Adding a Two-car Garage and Gaining a Family Room   171

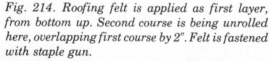

Fig. 213. *Portable circular saw is slid down roof decking, using flooring blade to trim shingles for insertion of aluminum flashing after roofing is applied. Flooring blade is hardened, less subject to damage if nails are contacted.*

Fig. 214. *Roofing felt is applied as first layer, from bottom up. Second course is being unrolled here, overlapping first course by 2". Felt is fastened with staple gun.*

Fig. 215. *Felt is bent down over decking edge at gable end. Upper sheathing hasn't yet been applied, will fit under decking.*

Fig. 216. *Roofing felt on rear pitch of roof, shingles on walls and barge board under roof at gable end. Soffit and fascia board will close rafter ends. Shingles come next.*

Fig. 217. As with roofing felt, shingling begins at
bottom, so successive courses can overlap to shed
rain. Ladder rests against front fascia board.
Shingles at gable end will be trimmed with trimming knife. After that, installation of garage doors
will complete the job. This one was done by
homeowner and family helpers.

Fig. 218. A year later. Old blacktop driveway has
been bulldozed, removed and replaced with lawn.
New crushed stone driveway has been power
rolled and blacktopped.

Adding a Two-car Garage and Gaining a Family Room   173

24

ADDING A ONE-CAR GARAGE AND GAINING TWO BEDROOMS AND A DEN

This addition provided a second garage, needed for a second car, a new master bedroom, a den that might later become a bath and an extra front bedroom. The same general plan could be followed with or without modifications in many raised ranch homes with a one-car garage. If the extra garage length added for the workshop isn't required, the addition could be built within the front-to-back dimensions of the house and still provide the added bedrooms.

In this instance, the homeowner did his own excavating for the footings, poured his own footings and built the foundation walls of masonry block. Professionals were hired to pour the slab floor of the garage. Much of the framing was a family project.

The forward portion of the roof is an extension of the main roof, with gables of matching pitch. The rear of the roof is lower pitched, covering the new master bedroom. Rafters of the rear portion start from the rear pitch of the main roof.

The original blacktop driveway was widened for part of the distance from garage to road. Access to the new garage and workshop is through a standard-width doorway cut in the outer wall of the original garage.

Fig. 219. Before. Typical raised ranch home with one-car garage. Cement mixer and supply of masonry blocks at right are in preparation for addition.

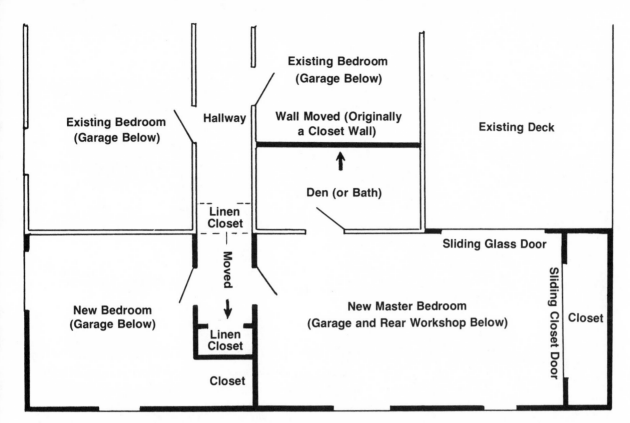

Existing Bedroom
(Garage Below)

Hallway

Existing Bedroom
(Garage Below)

Wall Moved (Originally
a Closet Wall)

Existing Deck

Den (or Bath)

Linen
Closet

Moved

New Bedroom
(Garage Below)

Linen
Closet

Closet

Sliding Glass Door

New Master Bedroom
(Garage and Rear Workshop Below)

Sliding Closet Door

Closet

Fig. 220. One-car garage below end bedrooms of this raised ranch was expanded by adding another garage with two bedrooms above it. Closet in existing bedroom was enlarged to become a den adjoining new master bedroom. Extra length of new garage provided workshop at rear.

Fig. 221. After. Second garage has been added at right, with workshop in rear, plus two bedrooms and a den on level above it. Driveway will be widened later.

Adding a One-car Garage and Gaining Two Bedrooms and a Den   175

Fig. 223. Rented cement mixer goes into action. Pile of sand in foreground, crushed stone pile behind mixer, will be mixed with portland cement to make concrete for footings that will support foundation of addition.

Fig. 222. First step. Trench has been dug for footing. Stakes in trench are marked for thickness of footing.

Fig. 224. Mixed concrete, poured from mixer, is leveled with hoe to proper footing thickness, then smoothed with float and trowel.

Fig. 225. *After leveling and smoothing, thickness stakes have been removed from footing. It's hard enough for first course of masonry block next day. Remainder of sand pile will be used in making mortar for block wall.*

Fig. 226. *The block job begins. First step is cleaning footing surface, applying mortar for first course of block.*

Fig. 227. *First two courses of block foundation wall have been laid. Concrete slab floor with iron mesh reinforcement is now being poured by pros, using mixer truck.*

Fig. 228. *Poured concrete slab is now being smoothed and leveled. Worker right is using rectangular wood float to smooth slab area next to house foundation. Worker at left is using long-handled float to smooth and level main slab area.*

Fig. 229. Completed garage floor, ready for further foundation wall construction.

Fig. 230. Foundation wall height increases. Note taut string atop blocks at right to keep block work in straight line and to assure that each course is level. Mortar is being applied to sidewalls of blocks in foreground.

Fig. 231. With wall completed, drainage tiles are laid at base to drain away ground water. Foundation wall has been coated with waterproofing material up to final grade level. Where excessive ground water is likely, Epoxy coating like Dur-A-Poxy 300 may be used for maximum seal.

Fig. 232. Framework for walls begins. Wall frame here extends overall height from foundation wall to upper floor level.

Fig. 234. Joists not yet installed serve as temporary floor above front of framing, to support plywood for subfloor.

Fig. 233. Floor joists for bedrooms are now placed, running fore and aft. Girder extends out from house in line with existing girder inside. Header above garage door opening supports front ends of front joists. Extra girder to rear of central one supports front ends of joists above rear workshop area. Plywood for subfloor is stacked on top of framing at left.

Fig. 235. Joists shown in Fig. 234 (used as temporary floor) are now being installed. Plywood subfloor in foreground is being nailed to joists already installed. View looking forward from rear of addition.

Fig. 236. With subfloor completed and lower framing sheathed, framing of upper floor is erected. Partial plywood covering on wall framing at upper right adds rigidity to framing while work progresses.

Fig. 237. Framing nears completion, with gabled roof already covered with plywood decking. Window openings have been framed in upper floor wall. Windows in lower wall were removed from existing house wall, reinstalled in addition, cutting costs.

Fig. 238. View from front of house as addition continues. First two courses of shingles have been applied over roofing felt at bottom of upper floor.

Fig. 240. Windows installed, shingling progresses. Insulation has been installed, and interior walls are now being completed.

Fig. 239. Entire addition is now sheltered. Shingles are being applied to end wall. Upper windows not yet installed.

25

ENLARGING A LIVING ROOM
AND ADDING A NEW BEDROOM

When more living room space was needed as toddlers grew to teenagers, this addition provided it, plus a new master bedroom with adjoining deck at the rear. A low headroom storage space under the addition also eases closet problems. The entire slab and foundation was done by professionals, as was the shell of the addition.

The project surmounted a weather problem, early snow, often encountered in late fall construction work. The major effect of the premature winter weather was a delay in the fireplace and chimney work.

A feature of the addition is the eye-appealing two-level living room with a step down from the old to the new—all new areas matching the old in color, flooring and trim. Outside, the roof line follows the step-down.

This, the second addition to the house, abuts an enclosed rear porch that began several seasons earlier as an open deck with storage under it. The enclosed porch, now a family room as planned, demonstrates an advantage to multi-stage add-ons. You gain living space at the completion of each phase without the inconvenience of prolonged construction time.

Fig. 241. Before. Remains of an early winter snow still show at right. Job began at start of winter.

Fig. 242. Floor plan of addition. Wall between old living room and new living room area is removed. Normal-height step joins the two floor levels.

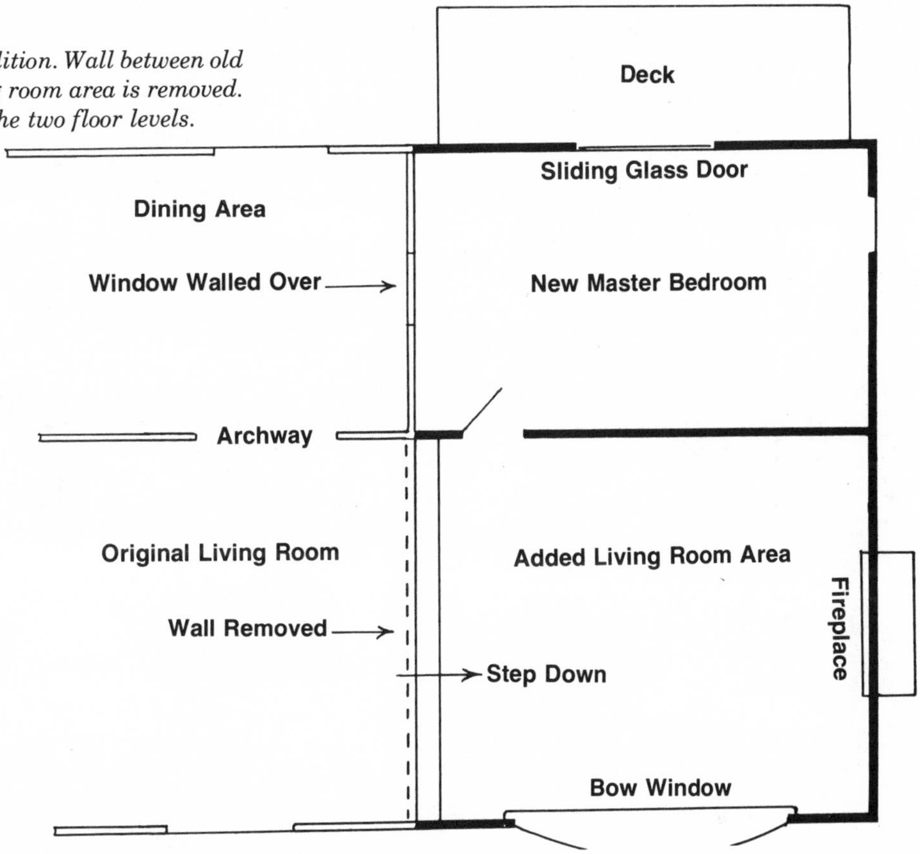

Deck

Dining Area

Sliding Glass Door

Window Walled Over →

New Master Bedroom

Archway

Original Living Room

Added Living Room Area

Wall Removed →

→ **Step Down**

Fireplace

Bow Window

Fig. 243. After. With new wing added, house looked like this the following summer.

Fig. 244. Inside, living room looked like this before addition. Railing shows in foreground at top of entrance stairway.

Fig. 245. After addition, greatly expanded living room looked like this immediately after job was completed. Stairway railing makes comparison easy.

Fig. 246. First step. Ground has been excavated, footings poured at site of addition next to house. Foundation will be built by professionals. Polyethylene sheeting covers footings, keeps them damp, protects them from rain or snow. Sheeting prevents too-rapid drying which could weaken concrete.

Fig. 247. Truck brings forms for foundations. These will be erected on hardened footings by foundation contractor.

Fig. 248. After foundation forms are erected, mixer truck brings concrete to fill them. Chute, leading from truck to forms, will carry concrete into forms under supervision of foundation contractor, as here.

Fig. 249. For low foundation walls, top of foundation is lower than top of form, so workmen level concrete below form tops. Stop-pieces are placed in forms where there are changes in foundation height.

Fig. 250. Here, forms have been removed after concrete hardened. Workmen scrape minor irregularities from foundation top. Note window openings at right, formed by blocking in forms.

Fig. 251. Framing is now built on foundation top. Low framed wall in foreground will be sheathed for shingling down to level of existing house. Girder is in place with rear joists on top of it. Snow has fallen since previous photo was taken.

Fig. 252. Front header has been set in place, installation of front joists has begun. (Front and rear joists overlap at girder.) Framing at fireplace location allows for hearth.

Fig. 253. Shingles are removed from area where added floor framing joins house, so framing members can be nailed directly through sheathing into house framing. Subflooring has been applied to floor framing.

Fig. 254. Walls are now erected. Sheathing was applied to wall framing beforehand. Gap at corner will be closed. Fireplace opening, temporarily closed, will be opened when fireplace construction begins.

Fig. 255. Roof is complete next. Entire addition is now sheathed with plywood. New roof is slightly lower than original to break ridge line.

Fig. 256. Rear of addition. Application of roof shingles has begun. Addition adjoins rear enclosed porch that began as shown in Figs. 258 and 259.

Fig. 257. Wall and roof shingling completed, bow window installed. Fireplace and chimney work begun, but must be keyed to weather.

Fig. 258. Rear enclosed porch began as open porch with corner posts on open deck attached to back of house and storage space enclosed under it. Back steps at right.

Fig. 259. Corner posts (4 x 4) plus intermediate studs at 16" spacing on centers were covered with $1/2$" plywood sheathing to enclose open deck. Roof is pitched $1/2$" per foot downward from house to rear wall, covered with roll roofing.

Fig. 260. Addition shown in Fig. 256 is now completed with deck extending from sliding bedroom doors. Deck abuts previously enclosed deck (Figs. 258, 259).

Enlarging a Living Room and Adding a New Bedroom   189

26

DOUBLING A ONE-CAR GARAGE

This addition expanded a one-car garage to a two-car one without unnecessary work. The trouble-saving feature was the extension of the gabled roof at a lower pitch than the original. This made it possible to start the new rafters from the existing ridge without any alterations to the other side of the roof. Verticals from the original outer wall of the existing garage reinforced the roof extension and provided a truss effect.

To provide easy passage between the old and the new, a section of the original outside garage wall was removed and topped with a header under the plate. Windows from the old wall were replaced in the outer wall of the new section. A new garage door, matched to the original, was used in the addition. The new rafters were spaced directly over the old ones and nailed through the existing roof into them.

Fig. 261. Before. One-car garage attached to house through enclosed breezeway.

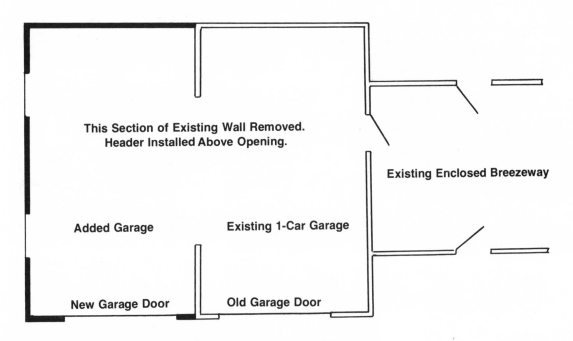

This Section of Existing Wall Removed. Header Installed Above Opening.

Existing Enclosed Breezeway

Added Garage

Existing 1-Car Garage

New Garage Door

Old Garage Door

Fig. 262. Garage area was doubled by adding new 1-car section to existing 1-car garage. Section of original garage's outer wall was removed to join old and new areas.

Fig. 263. After. Two-car garage has two roof pitch angles, simplifying job and cutting costs.

Fig. 264. First step. Low poured foundation wall was built on footings placed below frost line. Sill is already bolted to top of foundation wall. Note that sill lumber has been creosoted.

Fig. 265. Framing of outer side wall and rear wall are erected, braced with diagonals.

Fig. 266. Roof rafters are installed. At upper end, rafters are nailed through existing roof into original rafters, which remain. Uprights from eaves of original roof to new rafters will form a truss.

Fig. 267. Plywood sheathing is now applied over framing. Roofing felt covers roof decking. Asphalt roof shingles and wood wall shingles will complete the job.

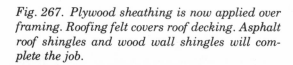

TOOLS YOU WILL NEED

FOUNDATION WORK

If you're in the habit of doing your own fix-it jobs around the house, the chances are you already have many of the tools required to remodel or add to your house. If you do your own foundation work, the methods you use will determine the tools you'll need, some of which should be rented. If you mix your own concrete on a major scale, as in pouring a floor or an extensive footing, for example, you can rent a cement mixer from a tool rental firm. You'll also need a wood float, which is like a large rectangular trowel, for rough-finishing the slab surface and a rectangular steel trowel for final smoothing. In general, however, you'll save time and work by using mixer-truck delivered concrete. Compare prices before you decide. If you'll be laying masonry block, you can mix your mortar in a wheelbarrow or garden cart. You'll need a hoe for the mixing job and mason's tools. These should include a large and small triangular trowel, a brick set, mason's hammer, and a tool called a "joiner"—the last one if you want very smooth mortar joints.

CARPENTRY

When the framing begins, the tools you'll use first are the measuring tools. You'll need a steel roll-up rule and one or more squares. If your square enables you to mark not only for right-angle cuts but also for 45-degree cuts, you'll be able to use it for mitering work when you get to the interior trim. Several such squares are shown in the photo. Stanley also makes a saw that can be used for squaring and miter marking (see Fig. 278).

The Electric Handsaw

For cutting your lumber to size, the tool you'll use most often is the portable circular saw. If you have to buy one, be sure it can cut through a 2 x 4, preferably not only at 90 degrees, but also at 45 degrees. One with a 7"-diameter blade can do the trick. A combination blade on the saw lets you cross-cut lumber to length or rip it to width when necessary. Most of your cutting will be to length. When you get to the interior work, especially built-ins, you'll need a

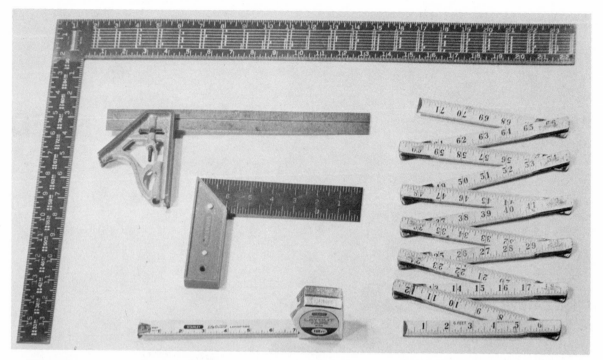

Fig. 268. Top to bottom, left: Rafter square. It's calibrated for marking rafter end cuts at precise angle for required roof pitch. Calibrations can also be used for laying out stair stringers. Tool can be used, too, as measuring straight edge and for squaring. This one's a Stanley sold with its own 48-page instruction booklet. Combination square below it has sliding handle, can be used for squaring, mitering, as depth gauge or try square, and as a level, as handle contains level tube. Below it, try and miter square can be used for squaring or miter marking. The 45-degree handle end is set against board edge for miter marking. Bottom: Roll-up steel tape rule. This is a Stanley Layout Tape, wider than average, rigid enough to extend across broad gaps in structure. Right: Zigzag folding rule. This one is also a rigid type. Available with brass extension slide in end section for measuring inside dimensions.

Fig. 270. Bevel gauge, often simply called a bevel. Set it to any angle you want to duplicate, then use it to mark the angle on anything you want to cut at the same angle. Very useful in roof and truss work.

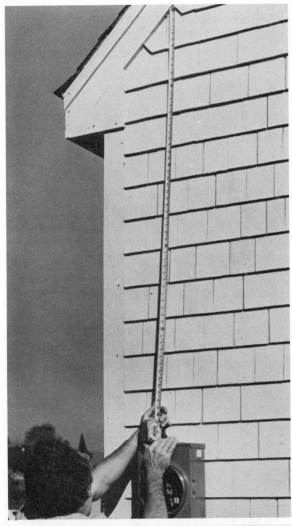

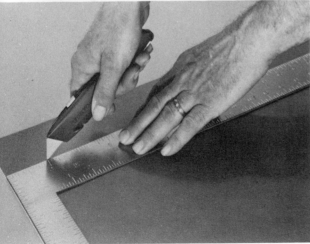

Fig. 269. *How stiff steel tape rule with brake (to hold it at fixed length) is used in typical measuring job. This one's a Stanley Powerlock.* STANLEY TOOL CO.

Fig. 271. *Levels are used in framing work to ascertain when horizontal members are truly horizontal and when vertical members are truly vertical. Bubble tube parallel to length of level gauges the horizontal. Tube at right angle to horizontal is tube that gauges vertical. Upper two levels also have angled tube for gauging 45-degree slant.* STANLEY TOOL CO.

Fig. 272. *Retractible blade trimming knife (with replaceable blades) cuts a variety of sheet materials including roofing felt, floor tiles, insulating board, linoleum. It also scores gypsum board for neat straight line break-off. This one's a Stanley.* STANLEY TOOL CO.

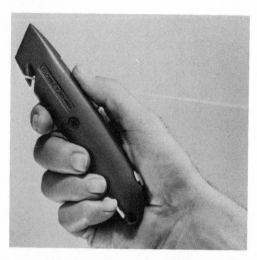

Fig. 273. Notch in bottom of this Stanley trimming knife cuts string or small cord cleanly, as in laying out and staking. Just retract the blade, slip string into notch and move blade forward for clean cut. STANLEY TOOL CO.

"plywood" blade. This is fine-toothed for cutting plywood and finish-grade lumber without fraying the fibers. You get a smooth, clean cut. But this is not the blade type for heavy framing work.

The Sabre Saw

The sabre saw is extremely useful in cutting holes through framing and sub-flooring for plumbing, wiring and duct work. If you have this type of work to do, select a saw with power and available blade length great enough to do the job reasonably fast. It need not be the highest priced saw on the list, but it probably won't be the lowest priced. The same type of saw is handy for much interior trim work, too. And, with metal-cutting blades it can cut your rain gutters and downspouts, as well as plumbing materials.

Fig. 274. Portable electric circular saw. Next to your hammer, you'll probably use this tool most in add-on or remodeling work. It has 7" diameter all-purpose blade for ripping or crosscutting.

Fig. 275. Sabre saw. Select one that will penetrate thickest material you'll have to cut through, typically subfloor plus sole, or a little more than 2". This one's a Stanley.

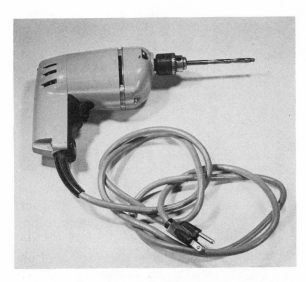

Fig. 276. Power drill. Either ¹/₄″ or ³/₈″ size will do. (Size is gauged by largest bit shank drill chuck can hold.) You'll need this tool to bore holes for wiring and plumbing, also to bore starting holes for sabre saw when cutting holes larger than can be done with drill alone.

The Power Drill

This tool serves many purposes. It can drill starting holes for screws, as in mounting certain types of electrical equipment, and it can bore larger holes, as required where pipes and cables pass through framing members. If it's to be used to bore holes through joists for water pipes, you'll be wise to buy a "right angle attachment" for the drill chuck. This enables you to bore holes in spaces otherwise too small for the drill to fit.

Drill size is designated by the maximum diameter bit shank that the drill chuck (which holds the bit) can accommodate. If the largest diameter the chuck can take is ¹/₄″, the drill is called a ¹/₄″ drill. If it can take a ³/₈″ diameter bit, it's a ³/₈″ drill. These two sizes are the most widely used. Naturally, either one can also take smaller-size bits down to ¹/₁₆″ or less, also such attachments as sanding disks, grooving cutters, hole saws (saws that cut large holes), etc.

Some power drills are of the usual grounded variety, with three-pronged plugs. Others are of "double insulated" construction with an outer shell of plastic and an internal design that shields all exterior metal parts from electric current. These have two-prong-plugs, offering convenience and additional electrical safety under certain conditions. Both types, however, are widely used.

The Hammer

A curved-claw nail hammer is the tool you'll use for most of your fastening work. If you'll be buying one for the job, make it a good quality one. The weight of a hammer is important, too, in building work. It's measured according to the weight of the hammer head. A popular weight for general work is 16 ounces, though for framing, many workers prefer a 20-ounce weight. The best bet is to pick the weight that feels comfortable to you. There's also a choice of handle materials, including wood, steel and fiberglass. Some pros choose wooden handles because they like the balanced "feel" that wood's light weight provides. If your hammer is likely to be subjected to marked humidity changes, however, favor one of the other handle types, such as tubular steel. The handle is rubber-sheathed for non-slip comfort. Naturally, steel doesn't swell or shrink with humid or dry weather. Actually, though, a high-quality hammer with any type handle isn't likely to develop trouble under normal conditions. So pick the one that feels best when you swing it.

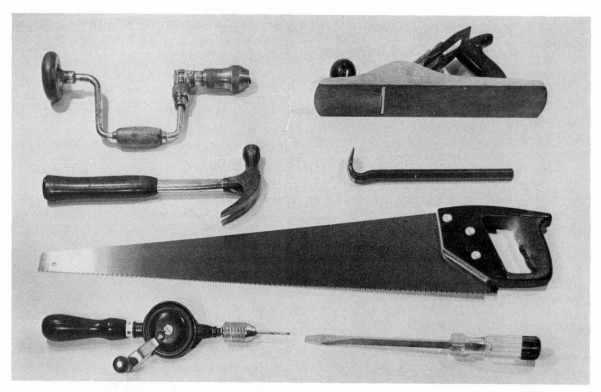

Fig. 277. The working tools. Left to right, top row: Bit brace takes various bit sizes for boring by hand, often a trouble saver. Jack plane, a handy tool in trim and interior work. Shaves over-width boards when required for fitting. Second row: Curved claw nail hammer. Does most of your fastening work in construction jobs. Nail puller and pry bar. Use it to get under head of misdriven nail hammer claws can't grab. A trouble saver. Next, handsaw. For use in spots hard to reach with power saw. Crosscut type is used most. Pick one with 7 or 8 teeth per inch. Ripsaw, for lengthwise cuts, has coarser teeth, typically $5^1/_2$ per inch. Bottom row: Hand drill makes holes up to $^1/_4''$ diameter in spots hard to reach with power drill, or beyond your cord length. Handy for pilot holes near lumber ends to prevent splitting. Screwdriver. You'll need several sizes for interior cabinetwork.

Handsaws

Even though you have an electric saw, there are times when a plain old handsaw is indispensable. It can, for example, fit into tight spots where an electric saw can't. And handsaws are relatively inexpensive. As in the case of the hammer, it pays to buy a good one. Since it's likely that you'll often have to cut damp wood (which tends to make a saw bind in the cut), you'll do well to choose a "taper ground" saw, even though it's more expensive than ordinary saws. This type has a blade that's actually thinner at the back (the edge opposite the toothed edge) and also at the tip than at the butt, or handle end. As a result, there is much less friction between the side surfaces of the blade and the wood, so it cuts faster and with less effort. Although shorter lengths are available, a 26″ blade is a good choice for general work.

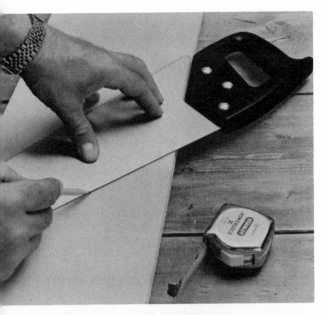

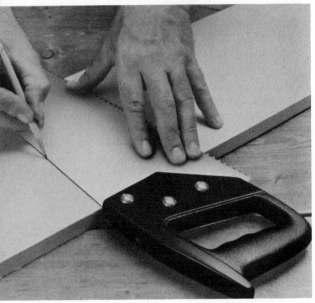

Fig. 278. Handle of this Stanley handsaw has edges that make it a marking tool, too. Top: It can be used for miter marking. Bottom: It's a square. After marking, it can make the saw cut along the marked line.

For interior work and trim, you'll find a miter box and backsaw or a miter-box saw (longer than the backsaw) very handy. In its simplest form the miter box is simply a wooden U-channel with slots in its sides to guide the saw blade. Typically, slots are provided to guide the saw for right-angle cuts and for 45-degree miter cuts. Simply place the wood to be cut in the U-channel, hold it firmly against one side and slide the saw back and forth in the slots to make the cut. The difference between a backsaw (or miter-box saw) and an ordinary handsaw is in the reinforced back edge, which is reinforced with a steel channel to keep the saw from flexing. This assures a straight cut. To assure a smooth cut edge, as required in interior trim work, saws of this type have finer teeth than most ripsaws and crosscut saws. Typically, backsaw types have from 11 to 13 teeth per inch. Crosscut handsaws usually range from 7 to 11 teeth per inch, ripsaws around 5½ teeth per inch.

Staplers

You're likely to need a stapler for a variety of jobs, such as installing insulation and anchoring building paper and roofing felt. Many types of weatherstripping also call for a stapler, as do many types of ceiling tile. When you buy your stapler, tell your supplier what kind of work you want to do with it. You'll need a larger one, for example, if you'll be mounting ceiling tiles than you would need for insulation. If you buy a large one, however, it will usually be designed to take either long or short staples, according to the work to be done. For insulation, you might use ¼" staples, for example; for ceiling tiles, ⁹⁄₁₆" staples. And you'll find many uses for your stapler

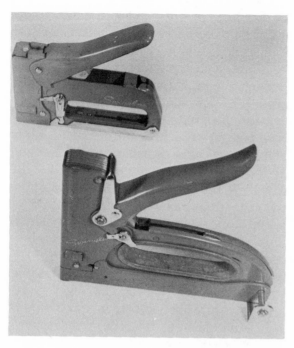

Fig. 279. Staple gun is used to fasten building paper, asphalt felt in preparation for roofing, and for installing fiberglass insulation and some types of ceiling tile. Select size that suits your needs. Large staple gun in foreground is Swingline model 900, can drive 9/16" staples for ceiling tiles. Smaller one in background is Swingline model 101 for lighter work, as installing insulation.

(as for your other tools) long after your building job is done.

WIRING TOOLS

For the wiring in your addition you'll need at least one screwdriver, slip-joint pliers and small-nosed pliers for the general work. The small-nosed pliers are used for shaping terminal loops in wire. You'll also be wise to buy an insulation stripping tool and a side cutter, which has handles like pliers and jaws with two meeting blades to cut wire. Electrician's pliers are

also handy. These have similar wire-cutting blades, plus flat jaws for bending heavy wire. If you're working with BX, you'll also need a hacksaw or metal snips, depending on what method you use to cut the metal covering. Both of these tools, like the others mentioned, will have many applications after the electrical work is completed. If your local code requires soldered connections for any part of the work, you'll also need a soldering iron. The handiest type is the electric soldering "gun," which heats up to soldering temperature faster than the old-style soldering iron.

PLUMBING TOOLS

The tools you need for your plumbing work (if any) depend on the type of pipe you use. For plastic, all you need is a saw (which you need for your framing work anyway), some sandpaper and the cement applicator that comes with the solvent cement. Your power drill, used for various operations in the building job, does the boring where water pipe runs through the framing. And your sabre saw cuts the holes for larger drain pipes. The power drill is used to make starting holes for the sabre saw.

If you're using copper pipe, you'll also need a tubing cutter for the small diameters (like water tubing), a hacksaw for larger diameters and a propane torch to provide the heat for the "sweated" soldered connections. If you're working in cold weather, especially on large-diameter copper pipe, you may need a second torch to provide the required heat. To remove the burrs from cut ends of tubing, you'll need a pipe reamer for the small diameters and a half-round file for the larger ones. Both of these tools are for smoothing the inside

Fig. 280 *What you need for wallboard work. Left to right, tools are: trimming knife (replaceable blade), curved-claw hammer, steel tape rule, broad putty knife. Shown below trimming knife: seam tape.*

ends of the cut. The flat side of the file can remove any roughness from the outside of the cut edge. You'll also need some fine sandpaper to clean the ends of the pipe before fluxing the joining portions of the pipe and the fitting.

For threaded pipe (if you use any), you'll need pipe-cutting and -threading tools. As these are not likely to have many applications after the job is done, it's usually advisable to rent them for the pipe sizes you'll need. The same applies to special tools required for certain types of cast iron pipe. Your best bet in planning for threaded steel or cast iron pipe is to first check with the plumbing supplier on the tools required. Then look for a tool rental agency that has the special tools you'll need.

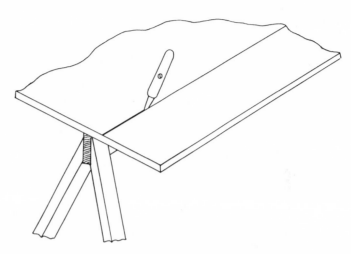

Fig. 281. *Score finish surface of wallboard with trimming knife, cutting through paper surfacing.*

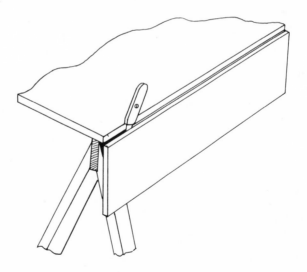

Fig. 282. *Press waste end of wallboard down over firm surface (like sawhorse), and gypsum breaks cleanly along scored line. Then use trimming knife to cut through paper on back surface of wallboard to separate cut-off waste piece.*

APPENDIX B

LIST OF SUPPLIERS

Andersen Windows
   Andersen Corporation
   Bayport, MN 55003

Armstrong Cork Co. (Flooring materials)
   Lancaster, PA 17604

Bird and Son (Roofing)
   East Walpole, MA 02032

Danbury Plumbing
   Danbury, CT 06810

Genova (Plastic pipe)
   Davison, MI 48423

Goldblatt Tools (Plasterer's tools)
   (Bliss Laughlin Industries)
   511 Osage
   Kansas City, KS 66110

Harvey Hubbell, Inc. (Electrical devices)
   State and Thomas Streets
   Bridgeport, CT 06602

Lord & Burnham (Greenhouses)
   Irvington-on-Hudson, NY 10533

Masonite Corp.
   Dept. TR-10
   Box 777
   Chicago, IL 60690

Mylen Industries (Spiral stairs)
   650 S. Washington St.
   Peekskill, NY 10566

Sonoco Products Co. (Sonotubes)
   Hartsville, SC 29550

Stanley Tools
   New Britain, CT 06050

Teco Wood Fasteners
   5530 Wisconsin Ave.
   Washington, DC 20015

Wiremold Co. (Raceway)
   West Hartford, CT 06110

INDEX